U.S. CHICANAS AND LATINAS WITHIN A GLOBAL CONTEXT

U.S. Chicanas and Latinas Within a Global Context

Women of Color at the Fourth World Women's Conference

Irene I. Blea

Westport, Connecticut
London

Library of Congress Cataloging-in-Publication Data

Blea, Irene I. (Irene Isabel)
U.S. Chicanas and Latinas within a global context : women of color
at the Fourth World Women's Conference / Irene I. Blea.
  p. cm.
  Includes bibliographical references and index.
  ISBN 0–275–95623–7 (alk. paper). — ISBN 0–275–95624–5 (pbk. :
alk. paper)
  1. Hispanic American women—Social conditions—Congresses.
2. Mexican American women—Social conditions—Congresses. 3. World
Conference on Women (4th : 1995 : Peking, China) I. Title.
E184.S75B58 1997
305.868—dc21   97–12806

British Library Cataloguing in Publication Data is available.

Library of Congress Catalog Card Number: 97–12806
ISBN: 0–275–95623–7
     0–275–95624–5 (pbk.)

First published in 1997

Praeger Publishers, 88 Post Road West, Westport, CT 06881
An imprint of Greenwood Publishing Group, Inc.

Printed in the United States of America

The paper used in this book complies with the
Permanent Paper Standard issued by the National
Information Standards Organization (Z39.48–1984).

10 9 8 7 6 5 4 3 2 1

Copyright Acknowledgments

Sandra Romero and Oscar Castillo have given permission to use several of the photographs in this book.

To Raven, to Hermanas Unidas, the homegirls,
to the Latinas I have had the pleasure of knowing
and loving

CONTENTS

TABLES AND FIGURES

INTRODUCTION

This text brings together two important elements of my recent past: my relocation to southern California, and my trip to China in 1995 to read my poetry and to give a presentation on the status of U.S. Chicanas and other Latinas at the United Nations Fourth World Women's Conference. Two years earlier, in August 1993, I had moved to California to chair the oldest Department of Chicano Studies in the United States. I took with me my treasured daughter, Raven, twenty-five years of experience in Chicano Studies, and far too many mementos of my homeland, New Mexico. Upon arrival at California State University at Los Angeles, in Los Angeles, I found few of the urban stereotypes hyped by the media, and instead encountered the most outstanding diverse group of Latinas. These women were students, artists, poets, homemakers, former farm workers, union activists, civil rights organizers, politicians, attorneys, and immigrants, both legal and illegal.

Their stories, their struggles, their successes have motivated me to re-examine an earlier publication of mine, *La Chicana and the Intersection of Race, Class, and Gender* (Praeger, 1991). In *La Chicana* I outlined the lives of Mexican-American females, most of them U.S. born. The present volume revisits the lives of those women, and engages in academic comparison and contrast of them, other U.S. Latinas, and women of minority status around the world. This book also extends the dominant issues at the U.N.-sponsored women's conference in order to place U.S. Latinas within the global context of women around the world. Thus, this text examines the concerns addressed at the United Nations' conference in Beijing, China, and focuses Latinas in one of the richest countries of the world, who originated from some of the most underdeveloped countries on the globe.

I also build on my two other books, *Toward a Chicano Social Science* (Praeger, 1988) and *Researching Chicano Communities: Social-Historical, Physical, Psychological, and Spiritual Space* (Praeger, 1995). In these two texts, I emphasized Chicano community within the context of space occupied in society and how that space came to be defined by Chicanos and the dominant culture, both internally and externally. I now proceed to do this with U.S. Latinas because women also exist in social-historical, physical emotional, and spiritual space.

This text shows that many U.S. Latinas are, for the most part, indigenous to the Americas and so cannot be considered immigrants. The word indigenous is used in place of Native American. The term *Americas* as used here denotes all of the Americas, North, Central, and South America, and not just the United States. Herein is a hint of how some Latinas do not recognize international borders. This lack of recognition is mostly in the spiritual sense. In reality, the border between the United States and Mexico profoundly affects all Latinas. Furthermore, the process of Latina immigration is thought to be driven by males; it often is not. Those women who cross the boundaries endure extraordinary consequences. The boundaries are more than political; they are also social, psychological, and spiritual in nature, and they confine, constrict, and define women into remaining in "their place."

I have met women who have endured war and crossed male-dominated boundaries in Los Angeles, Europe, Mexico, Israel, and now in China. I have interviewed them with regard to their perspectives and expectations of the United States, their experiences in their own country, and the realities of living everyday life in the United States. For U.S. Latinas, the Americanization process, contemporary cultural roles, their hopes and dreams for the future, their visits to their homelands, and their people are the center of their lives.

This book updates the scholarship on the relationship between race or ethnicity, class, and gender by intersecting immigrant status, sexual orientation, and age. Accordingly, I analyze language and labels such as immigrant, nonimmigrant, Americano, Latina, and lesbian, and examine how these labels have unified some elements of the U.S. Latina community. But more than this, I focus on how they have also fragmented that community and discuss a Latina feminist agenda in the United States. This book explores the fragmentation of the U.S. women's movement, describes the nature of the countries from which Latinas originated, and reviews U.S. interaction with those countries. It also reviews the appearance of Chicanas and other Latinas on the national and international scene in the major social institutions of politics, health, economics, education, religion, and criminal justice. Furthermore, it examines the shared lives of U.S. Latinas with other American women—white, African-American, and indigenous women—and how women can integrate a Latina feminist perspective into the global women's movement.

Chapter 1 discusses the goals and objectives of the U.N. Fourth World Women's Conference. It documents the lack of Chicana participation in the first U.N. conference in 1975, held in Mexico City, and explores the role of nongovernmental organizations at the U.N. conference. It introduces the reader to China, the host country of the 1995 conference, and to the idea of feminizing racism, which was my primary reason for attending the conference.

Chapter 2 details how Chicanas have historically struggled to relate to the U.N. conference and the platform. Some of this difficulty has been attributed to the Mexican and U.S. border, which was created as a result of a vicious war and has created intense racial divisions. This chapter addresses these divisions by introducing the Chicano and Chicana civil rights movement, and links it to the U.N. platform on human rights for women.

Chapter 3 profiles U.S. Latinas by presenting demographic data and addressing issues of physical, psychological, spiritual, and social space. Chapter 4 traces how the evolution of Chicana feminist consciousness is akin to the need for cultural sovereignty. This chapter studies Chicana cultural icons such as la Virgen de Guadalupe, la bruja, la curandera, and la llorona. Chapter 5 challenges the Chicana colonial legacy and strives to feminize racism. One of its primary contentions is that while men make war and women endure it, women and the rape of women are not calculated as part of the statistics on the casualties of war. Rarely is rape considered a war crime.

Chapter 6 contemplates how Chicanas have resisted and survived the Americanization process of their culture. It also explains Chicana sensitivity to the oppressed people of the world. Chapter 7 deals with U.S. expansionist politics and Chicana resistance to the Americanization process. Chapter 8 reviews the Chicana feminist movement and the development of the Chicana ethnic, gender, and racial political consciousness. Finally, Chapter 9 maintains that contemporary immigrant Latinas have inherited a legacy from U.S.-Mexican relations. This legacy, a Chicana/Chicano legacy, has severely challenged the centralization of whiteness and male dominance.

This text therefore demonstrates the concepts of Chicana power and leadership in transforming institutions, including the centralization of heterosexuality. It gives voice to how contemporary Chicana feminists have redefined their personal selves by redefining certain concepts, communication, and even their spirituality. This book illustrates the need to redefine womanhood by redefining the girl child as well as the rapidly aging Chicana baby boomers.

As part of the final focus of the U.N. conference, I discuss Beyond Beijing, the global women's movement that is seeking to take the work done in China to the barrios and ghettos, the suburbs and inner cities, wherever women live. In the current U.S. feminist discussions on multiculturalism, little notice has been given to the fact that multiculturalists are advocating what Chicanas and other women of color in the United States have demanded for more than thirty years since the civil rights movement began. At this time, multiculturalism may not be in the best interests of Chicanas, especially since most jobs relating to multiculturalism are going to white women. Until U.S. white women deal effectively with the fact that they are the global minority, until they deal effectively with racism, and until Chicanas are recognized as having first advocated, and then broken, old barriers to multiculturalism, the U.S. women's movement will be stifled. This book aims to strengthen that movement by emphasizing the fact that the global women's movement is populated by women of color. They are the global majority, and U.S. Latinas are certainly among them.

U.S. CHICANAS
AND LATINAS
WITHIN A GLOBAL CONTEXT

1

THE UNITED NATIONS FOURTH WORLD CONFERENCE ON WOMEN

Various countries at the United Nations Fourth World Conference in 1995 noted that the traditional view of women has concentrated on women's attraction, beauty, and motherhood. Through the ages special attention has been paid to her nude body, although in the United States some attention has recently been called to male bodies. Although U.S. images of women have changed from decade to decade, essentially their sexual relationship to men has remained paramount. Thus, we have witnessed the 1920s flapper, the risque modern female of the 1930s, and the loyal American worker during the early 1940s, filling in for her man during World War II—all of these images revolving around their sex. After the war, in the 1950s, the middle-class housewife became the leading popular image. She now stayed at home cooking and cleaning and watching television.

As stated, throughout U.S. history women have been defined in terms of their sexual relationship to men. Wives had sex with husbands, not with other women, and men were/are not supposed to have sex with their daughters, just as brothers are not supposed to have sex with their sisters or any other closely related female. In the 1960s, the American woman revolted against being defined by her sexual relationship to one man and opted for free sex without commitment. Women also resisted the message that catching a man and marrying him was the most important goal in life. It was not until the late 1960s and the 1970s that the

BLEA

Irene I.

Globa Focus

36830 • **United States of America**

When NGO women arrived in Beijing, China, they were instructed to wear their VIP identification tags at all times. Photograph taken upon arrival at the NGO conference.

United States recognized that it had a population of ethnic women who wanted much more, liberation from racism. It took the civil rights movement to make this clear to mainstream America. Foremost among these women of color are U.S. Latinas, who over the years have had a growing interest in the media and in international affairs, and more specifically, in the international conferences on women sponsored by the United Nations.

WORLD ATTENTION TO WOMEN

The United Nations International Conference on Women focuses on expanding human rights for women around the world. To date, four such conferences have been held: at Mexico City, Mexico, in 1975; at Copenhagen, Denmark, in 1980; at Nairobi, Kenya, in 1985; and at Beijing, China, in 1995. Over a thirty-year period, these conferences have been working to develop a human rights platform for the United Nations that defines and protects women's rights throughout the world. At the 1985 conference, the General Assembly adopted and ratified the Forward Looking Strategies (FLS) for the Advancement of Women. The document consists of 372 recommendations that are scheduled for implementation by governments by the year 2000. The platform covers policies ranging from the rights of immigrant women (Paragraph 301) to counting women's unwaged (unpaid) work (Paragraph 120). The September 1995 conference in Beijing was to assess the progress made by governments in implementing the FLS recommendations, to develop new areas, and to prioritize issues within a document, the Platform of Action (PFA), that would come from the conference. The PFA is a report on the programs recommended to the United Nations. In Beijing, the original world effort was extended to go beyond the year 2000 in order to ensure that obstacles to women would not persist into the next century. These rights identified by women for women include the protection of immigrant women (an issue of special importance to Latinas), counting women's unpaid labor, fighting domestic violence and genital mutilation, and alleviating poverty. Aside from reading my poetry and addressing the status of U.S. Latinas at the conference, I attended the conference in order to feminize racism—that is, to make it a feminist issue just as poverty has become a feminist issue.

In 1975, the U.N. General Assembly proclaimed International Women's Year. The year was to be devoted to intensified action designed to promote equality between men and women, ensure the integration of women into the total development effort, and increase women's contribution to world peace. The World Conference of the International Women's Year was convened in Mexico City, and many participants identified themselves strongly with the themes of equality, development, and peace. This effort materially helped develop feminism worldwide. International Women's Year was followed by the United Nations' Decade for Women: 1976–1985. In turn, the "decade" was followed by the creation of two U.N. bodies devoted exclusively to women: UNIFEM and INSTRAW. UNIFEM, the United Nations Development Fund for Women, was originally called the United Nations Voluntary Fund for Women and concentrated on innovative development activities that would benefit women, especially in rural regions of the developing world. INSTRAW, the International Research and Training Institute for the Advancement of Women, supports the fuller participation of women in the economic, social, and political spheres. (See *Women, Challenges to the Year 2000,* 1991, New York: United Nations). On December 18, 1979, the United Nations adopted the Convention on the Elimination of All Forms of Discrimination against Women in the General Assembly, which has been described as the women's Bill of Rights. This convention entered into force on September 3, 1981, and has now been ratified by over 100 nations, though not by the United States.

The World Conference to Review and Appraise the Achievements of the United Nations Decade for Women was held in Nairobi, Kenya, in July 1985. This conference drew 16,000 delegates and representatives from roughly 28,000 nongovernmental organizations (NGOs). That year, all participating governments adopted by consensus the Nairobi Forward-looking Strategies for the Advancement of Women to the Year 2000. This was to be a blueprint for women's future that identified specific areas for action by governments and the international community to improve the status of women over the fifteen years until the year 2000 (p. 2). In 1990, the Commission on the Status of Women undertook a five-year review to appraise the implementation of the Nairobi Forward-looking Strategies. It found that women's situation had deteriorated in many parts of the world, especially in developing countries.

The convocation at Mexico City was a rude awakening for U.S. women. The first global conference ever held on women was attended by 133 international states and more than 1,000 delegates. U.S. women discovered that there were other Americans in the hemisphere and that they had some serious differences. In preparation for the conference, they also discovered that their feminist agenda did not speak for all women in their country, especially Chicanas, African Americans, Asians, and indigenous women. White women ignored what women of color in their own country told them in the United States and had to go to Mexico to discover that Chicanas had more in common with women outside of their country than within it. At this conference, white U.S. women found themselves in the minority.

When the international discussion on women continued in August 1995, some of the same issues emerged. Now, however, intensified effort was made to get women protection under the law—that is, the legacy of tradition, especially in marriage, equality and the difference between theory and practice, equality in the law. The conference was not without controversy. The first matter to be considered was the location of the conference. NGO women around the world were prepared to hold their conference in Beijing in order to lobby the U.N. delegates. The NGO conference was organized in order to hold the official United Nations delegation accountable for the decisions they made and for how these decisions affected women. In this way, issues were taken out of the men's control, and women became involved in the governmental process, no longer relegated to being merely the recipients of policy.

At the last minute the NGO conference was moved to Huairou, near the Great Wall, more than an hour away from Beijing. Women bombarded the Chinese government with requests to move the conference back to Beijing, but they were unsuccessful. Women were suspicious of the reason why it had been moved. The Chinese government contended that it could not accommodate 30,000 women in Beijing at the same time that the U.N. conference was taking place. In addition to the NGO women, the government said, there would be U.N. delegates, security people, tourists, and reporters. For their part, many women contended that the conference was moved in order to prevent the world from seeing such a large gathering of women addressing issues defined by women. Some of those issues included the outlawed Chinese tradition of binding women's feet and killing girl babies. In short, the Chinese government wanted to isolate the women and keep their issues away from the U.N. delegates and international attention.

Thus, the conference began with considerable dissatisfaction, which only escalated once the women were checked into the conference in Beijing, given three by five inch identification tags, and escorted to the Huairou site. Identification tags were supposed to give the women VIP status but instead served to isolate them further. It was reported that the Chinese people were instructed to keep away from the delegates to either conference. They were to be courteous and to answer only general information questions concerning directions and the acquisition of services. Those with automobiles were instructed to drive them on even- or odd-numbered days, depending on their license plate number. The streets of Beijing and Huairou were cleaned, and no honking was allowed so that China could present a neat and orderly appearance to the world.

Even though buses were provided for free to get the women to and from Huairou, most U.S. women were uncomfortable in the dirty vehicles, which leaked when it rained, and whose ride was at best rough. Most U.S. Latinas, accustomed to "Third World" transportation and poor accommodations during the rain, displayed a larger comfort zone. All the women, however, were impressed by the bicycle as China's primary mode of transportation. The "official" buses did not deviate from the well-constructed, tree-lined "official" roads and streets, and the daily trip to Huairou offered little opportunity to see the rural areas away from the road. Sightseeing was done mostly by tour bus and was limited to the well-established tourist sites, which included trips to pearl, cloisonné, and tile factories where U.S. dollars and credit cards were honored.

It is difficult to select which was the most interesting, or impressive aspect of visiting China. Learning took place by comparison. For example, traditional Chinese architecture in Beijing was frequently photographed because it reminded Chicanas and Mexicanas of the Aztec temple of Quetzalcoatl outside of Mexico City. Also, the average Chinese citizen appeared to be about the average height of most Latinas. Chinese skin color was familiar; but frequent comments were made about how Latinas tended to have larger (fatter, heavier) bodies.

It was reported that the Chinese government expected women at the conference to "propagandize" Chinese women with feminism. U.S. women were among the most radical attendees and were certainly to be kept at a distance from Chinese women. Another report that circulated was that the Chinese government expected women to demonstrate in the nude near Mao's tomb in Tiananmen Square. The rumor was that government officials were ready to cover the women with t-shirts and bed sheets and haul them away. No such demonstrations were planned, and none took place.

Chinese and English were the official languages of the conferences, but few Chinese women were visible at the conference. Because our efforts to initiate contact resulted in the intimidation of Chinese women, we stopped initiating contact with regular citizens and concentrated on those who contacted us. We did not want to get women on the street into trouble. While we would eventually leave China, they would still be there to face the consequences of our actions. Reportedly, the Chinese government warned their citizens not to interact with the women of the conference, especially U.S. women. They were to answer questions regarding directions and services only. They were to be polite and move away quickly. At the NGO conference, some translation was provided. Mainstream U.S. women did not cope well with the constant surveillance; some were convinced that their rooms were searched when they were at the conference.

THE PLATFORM

The Platform for Action identifies critical concerns that present obstacles to women's advancement around the world. These concerns are human rights concerns defined as women's rights, and they go beyond family and parenting rights to include rights for girls, young women, and older women, especially if they impact governmental policy and programs for or about women. Reduced to its simplest form, the Platform pronounced that violence against women in all its forms must stop; girls must be protected and valued equally with boys; women must have access to education and high-quality health care in a way that is relevant to women; women must have access to economic and political power; men must share family responsibility; women have the right to control

Chinese architecture in Beijing reminded U.S. Chicanas and Mexicanas of the Aztec temple of Quetzalcoatl outside of Mexico City.
Photograph by Irene I. Blea.

their own fertility; women have the right to participate equally in sexual relations; and women must be guaranteed freedom of expression.

At the United Nations conference, the United States committed itself to action in major areas of the Platform, and following the meeting, moved to establish a President's Interagency Council on Women to plan effective implementation of the Platform. An office was set up in the White House, and a telephone number (202) 456–7350 was assigned. The Council is developing a National Action Agenda to move the United States toward the goals of the United Nation Conference on Women by the year 2000. It is to develop a report of successful actions in local communities, as suggested by the Platform for Action (Paragraph 297) which encourages countries to develop a nation plan on women. Members of communities are encouraged to participate, and the Council can be contacted via fax (202) 456–7337 or via e-mail through their web site (http://www.whitehouse.gov/WH/EOP/Women/IACWhome.html).

The United States also committed itself to implementing the Working Women Count Honor Roll, a campaign to improve conditions for women in the workplace as part of the Women's Bureau of the Department of Labor. Other platform issues included security for women, defined as freedom from domestic violence, rape, and sexual harassment. Other considerations under this topic included gun control, law enforcement, treatment in the judicial system, prisons, new methods of conflict resolution, diplomacy, peacemaking, peacekeeping, and the elimination of violence in the media. The U.S. commitment included increasing women's economic security by recognizing leaders in the micro-lending field and ensuring funding by federal agencies. As part of the security measures, the United States also propelled a six-year $1.6 billion initiative to fight violence against women. Addressing violence against women means addressing issues of peacekeeping, weapons, and war.

The U.S. plan is to improve women's health, especially that of women of color, throughout their life cycle. This is especially important as a large number of women who were born during the baby boom begin to age. The additional problems of low-income women and those from ethnic and racial backgrounds are also considered. Women's health care and services are of prime importance and go beyond family planning services and reproductive rights to include gender-specific conditions such as menopause, pregnancy, breast cancer screening, aging, teen pregnancy, and AIDS. Disease prevention has become health promotion, and includes issues of health insurance, violence, and environmental impacts.

Educational barriers faced by women, including those with disabilities, are also a great concern. Women of color in particular are lobbying the U.S. Senate to ratify the U.N. Convention on the Elimination of All Forms of Discrimination Against Women (CEDAW) in education and all other fields. The U.S. plans for women in international development are to

Table 1.1
Occupational Stratification by Gender and Ethnicity

	Hisp.F.	Hisp.M.	Non.Hisp.F.	Non.Hisp.M.
Farming, forestry fishing	1.6	7.3	0.8	3.6
Operators, fabricators laborers	15.2	28.1	7.2	19.2
Services	23.5	16.1	17.0	10.2
Technical, sales administrative support	39.1	16.7	44.8	21.5
Managerial, Professional	17.0	28.2	28.2	27.4

Source: U.S. Department of Commerce, Bureau of the Census. *We the American Hispanics.* November, 1993, p. 8.

increase women's political participation and promote knowledge about women's legal rights. As part of the international development focus, the country is committed to a micro-enterprise program to enable low-income women entrepreneurs in developing countries to gain access to credit. Finally, the United States has pledged support to improving the health and well-being of women in developing countries, and it continues an initiative, announced at the World Summit for Social Development in March 1995, to increase girls' primary school completion rate at the international level (Table 1.1).

Other exciting possibilities have arisen. For example, in the spring of 1994, the Women's Bureau of the U.S. Department of Labor surveyed working women across the country seeking to establish how they felt about their jobs and what they wanted to change. More than a quarter of a million women responded to the Working Women Count survey. Working women maintained that they needed change in three areas: getting better pay and benefits, balancing work and family, and gaining more respect and opportunity on the job. A Working Women Count Honor Roll program has been established to encourage employers to make concrete changes in the lives of working women and their families. The program's goal is to obtain more than a thousand pledges affecting the lives of at least a million working people in the next year. Employers are finding that the Honor Roll programs benefit workers, and at the same time increase productivity and thus company profits. Women can gain access to empowering formation by contacting the Women's Bureau of the U.S. Department of Labor, as well as the President's Interagency Council of Women at the White House. In addition, a series of publications on the U.N. Fourth World Conference on Women has been issued.

The conference gave women an opportunity to redefine what traditionally had been referred to as social problems. With regard to economic issues, for example, homemakers are now conceptualized as unwaged laborers. Not being paid for labor keeps women poor. Other economic concerns for women include welfare reform, corporation and government downsizing or restructuring, retirement, the glass ceiling (that is, the appearance of upward mobility but no actual mobility), minimum wage, wages and benefits, pay equity, working conditions, the North American Free Trade Agreement (NAFTA), free markets, child care, elder care, women-owned businesses, microenterprise, the gap between rich and poor, the environment, and the impact of environmental degradation on the poor.

Under the broad discussion of opportunity and discrimination, there is attention to education, job training, retraining, computer literacy, legal literacy, affirmative action, job development, all forms of discrimination such as that which influences immigration policy, refugees, and religious freedom. Entities designed to advance the status of women, such as the Interagency Council, Commissions on the Status of Women, various governmental and nongovernmental offices, and independent groups, have emerged as a result of the U.N. Conference. The right to advance the status of women is guaranteed by CEDAW, Title IX of the Education Amendments of 1972, and Title VII of the Civil Rights Act of 1964.

Of primary importance to women is their health, which can be defined as a vital prerequisite of human rights, especially during pregnancy. At the conference it was revealed that between 1950 and 1980 female health improved substantially as a result of clean water, better sanitation, and improved primary health care; nutrition has improved through the global perspective on women stimulated by the international conferences. Latinas involve themselves seriously in health issues, especially in South America where women still die during childbirth. As of 1983, roughly 275 women in Latin America and the Caribbean died per 100,000 live births.

Finally, serious attention is being paid to developing leadership among women through participation in governmental activities around the world. More women are running for elective office and are seeking appointments to positions, boards, and commissions. To assist in this effort, new networks and communication vehicles have been adopted to change women's status and image. Latinas, both within and outside of the United States, however, still remain out of the mainstream of the United States' technological movement. Although many advances have been made, most federally funded positions concerned with women's issues have gone to white women. Some black women have been placed in leadership roles, but Latinas are rarely visible; certainly, they are not represented in proportion to their percentage of the population.

LATINAS AND THE U.N. PLATFORM

What does the platform mean to Latinas? According to the United Nations' World Survey on the Role of Women in Development report of 1985, Latin America's progress in legal provisions and public opinion in favor of allocating resources to be used in favor of women is on the rise. All South American countries, with the exception of Suriname, have ratified the Convention on the Elimination of All Forms of Discrimination Against Women. Brazil's new constitution has abolished discrimination against women with regard to land ownership, social security benefits, and retirement. Colombia is considering legislation that will redefine part-time work and maternity leave. In Nicaragua, legislation stipulates that both parents must share the responsibilities of raising children and doing housework. These improvements are credited to the U.N. conference on women (Fisher, 1989).

As a result of the international focus on women, school enrollment has increased in Latin America. Among Latin American and Caribbean women, the percentage rate of illiterate women 20 to 24 years of age was only about 8.5 percent in 1990 compared to 20 percent in 1970. In 1970, the illiteracy rate was lower than that of eastern and southeastern and southern Asian women, and it was especially low compared to Africa's rate. Especially illiterate and undereducated are rural women. Illiteracy goes beyond reading and writing. Women have largely been kept culturally illiterate. The 1995 women's conference demonstrated that social change had indeed taken place. School attendance and adult literacy rates were much higher in Latin American countries than in other developing countries, for both females and males. Compared with women in Africa and the Middle East, Latin American women have had a relatively long history of participation in higher education. In Chile, women were permitted to enter universities by presidential decree in 1877. That right was not first established for Saudi women until almost a century later. Girls in all developing countries who live in rural areas have the worst chance of any sector of the world's population to get even a primary school education. In urban areas, girls generally have fewer opportunities than boys to attend secondary school and universities. A higher proportion of girls than boys drop out of educational facilities at all levels in countries as different as Mexico, Ghana, Kenya, and Pakistan.

At the conference, Latinas from the Americas met women who were very much unlike themselves. Among the most interesting to them were the Muslim women who spoke about the role of women according to the Koran, their holy book of scripture. This text is the source of traditional religion in Islamic countries. Islamic women explained that Mohammed, the author of the Koran, wanted to improve the lot of Arab women, who until Mohammed's decree in the seventh century A.D., had been given in marriage by men. Women had no property rights, and only the husband could call for divorce. The Koran requires that men respect women and treat them fairly, especially in the case of inheritance.

In the twentieth century, Muslim women pressured for the reform of laws affecting family life via the Personal Status Laws, which are concerned with marriage, divorce, and child custody. Koranic law allows men to have up to four wives at a time without their needing to gain the permission of any of their other wives. However, the Koran maintains that a man should not marry additional wives unless he can treat them equally. As Muslim feminists maintain, it is impossible for anyone to treat four people equally in every respect. Polygyny, the practice of having more than one wife, is illegal in Tunisia, Turkey, and the Muslim states of the former Soviet Union. In 1978, Syria required that a husband prove in court his ability to support additional wives. Most Muslim countries now require that men show good cause for divorce. Some countries now require men to pay their divorced wives money toward their support for a short period, sometimes up to a year. A 1975 law in Iran placed men and women of an equal basis in matters of divorce, but this law was repealed by the revolutionary government in 1979 (Fisher, 1989). Women's rights are almost nonexistent in Iran today.

U.S. LATINAS AND THE PLATFORM

Few observers give much attention to Latinas in the United States. The mass media have projected images of immigrants, but few images that demonstrate them as indigenous, original settlers, coping and thriving. In fact, a conservative U.S. Census figure (1993) estimates that at least 64 percent of all Latinos in the United States were born in this country. About half of those who were foreign born came to the United States between 1980 and 1990 from all over the Americas. Mexicans were the largest population, followed by Puerto Ricans, Cubans, Central Americans, and then South Americans, who represented nearly 5 percent. Dominicans, Spaniards, and other Latinos each accounted for over 2 percent of the Latino population.

Latinos are the fastest growing segment of the U.S. population, containing a higher proportion of young adults and children than the rest of the country. The population has the smallest number of elderly, and a disproportionate number of the elderly are women. In 1990, most Latinos lived in family households; about 70 percent of Latino families were maintained in married households; 9 percent of the families were headed by a male with no wife present and 22 percent by a female with no husband present. The median family income was lower than that of all Americans combined—$25,064 compared to $35,225.

The media and the dominant conception of reality must be transformed in order to end stereotypes. It is also necessary to include more positive images of Latinas instead of as being plagued by problems or generally as a social problem. The emphasis on youth and whiteness in the United States tends to feed the view that ethnicity and aging are problems. In developing the U.N. Platform, the conferences traced the history of women in many countries. The Platform placed that change within the context of male-dominated history but not without engaging in a sociological analysis. In isolation, a focus on women by younger generations does not recognize the need for change, and those generations get trapped in the same perspectives.

The 1975 conference in Mexico City was held during the United Nations Decade for Women between 1975 and 1985. When I first learned about the impending international conference on women in Mexico City, I was a graduate student completing work on a Ph.D. in Sociology at the University of Colorado in Boulder, and was highly active in the Chicano civil rights movement. Both as a student raising a child alone and as a woman of color, I found it difficult to enter the network of women who had information on the first conference, and I found it impossible to attend the Mexico City meetings because of the social and historical conditions in which I found myself. I had no money and no outside support to attend the conference. Information about the conference was difficult to obtain because the sources of information were scattered and controlled by white middle-class women attached to powerful men. When I finally identified sources with the information, then access became an immense issue. These sources did not freely give the details or space on any agenda. Nevertheless, I felt I had to tell my story and that of my daughter. My mother and father took care of my daughter. I scraped together every cent I could from various sources, and an undergraduate student took me to the airport, where I caught a fifty dollar round trip flight from Denver to El Paso, boarded a second-class bus, and endured the grueling eighteen-hour ride to Mexico City. Repeating virtually this same experience when the Nairobi conference convened, I vowed that the next conference call would be different. For this reason I kept informed and in touch with those "in the know" about forums that directly affect the quality of my life and the lives of millions of women like me.

I never knew the Copenhagen conference was taking place. When the Nairobi conference was announced for 1985, I was sitting on the National Board of the YWCA in the United States. I made an application to the executive committee, which would review the applications and provide the funds needed to take a representative group of multicultural women to Nairobi. Much political scrambling ensued, and east coast white and black women dominated the politics. It soon became apparent that the committee saw multiculturalism and diversity as a black–white issue, and mostly black and white women were supported. I did not attend.

Other women felt disempowered when they tried to address the international platform on women's human rights. For this reason, the NGO was established. It has evolved as a lobbying group to the United Nations conference, and it holds its conferences at the same time that the United Nations delegates meet to discuss women's rights. NGO was formed to hold the official delegation accountable for its decisions, thereby attempting to take the issues out of the control of women who were connected to powerful men, and to keep themselves involved in the governmental process. Nongovernmental organizations are not part of the government, but sometimes are affiliated with the government. As a Chicano civil rights activist, I have been involved in nongovernmental agencies for more than thirty years now. Thus, being attracted to the fourth NGO conference in Beijing was a natural evolution.

In 1975 (and today as well), Chicanas needed to involve themselves in nongovernmental agencies because of the racism, sexism, and poverty to which they were subjected. As persons of color in a highly stratified, postcapitalist society, Latinas and Latinos were, and still are, underrepresented in their government, in educational and economic structures, and in the health, religious, and spiritual bodies of the country. These women, however, are overrepresented in the most powerless positions of these institutions and the criminal justice system. A few Latinas engaged in personal boycotts against the U.N. Women's Conference, but decisions still were made with them. In my opinion, it is better to participate in bringing about change by working internally.

Latinas were especially sympathetic to Harry Wu, a dissident who was released by Chinese authorities upon our arrival in China. Wu had been imprisoned for spying on the Chinese government and for reporting on human rights violations. At that time much discussion took place among a diverse group of women about China's political need to demonstrate to the world its leniency toward political dissidents. This subject, however, was one of much contention as we observed that we were watched, videotaped, and followed. At the reception center we were instructed to wear large, three by five identification tags with our photo on them. As noted earlier, we were told that we would get VIP service if we wore the tag. The tags did indeed make us conspicuous. At our hotel there was a person on each floor to serve us, guard us, or keep track of us, depending on whose perspective was being sought. Some women reported that their rooms had been entered and searched. Women from Tibet drew special attention because of the political controversy between the Chinese government and Tibet. These women were closely monitored by the Chinese, as refugee women distributed multicolored lapel ribbons asking people to exert pressure on the Chinese government to get out of Tibet. The Chinese have been accused of human rights violations there, especially in the form of kidnapping, torture, rape (especially of nuns), massacres, and various forms of religious desecration. Some of the women at the conference had been exiled to other countries, while some parroted the Chinese party line testifying to how much they have benefited from the Chinese occupation. Chinese men took lots of pictures of them as they maintained they wanted to rule their own country.

DEFINING LA CHICANA

The theme of the NGO conference was "Looking at the World Through Women's Eyes." Most women watched the Chinese world from buses on tours or from their hotel rooms. The NGO conference began just prior to the Beijing U.N. conference and continued into the U.N. conference, thus, letting the U.N. delegates know that grassroots women were present and that their concerns needed to be addressed.

It was important that the world know that a fairly large group of conquered women known as Chicanas lived in one of the richest countries in the world, the United States, and that this group was among the poorest, most overworked, undereducated, and yet creative group of colonized women on the globe. After returning from the conference, I decided to document my presentation on U.S. Latinas, and compare and contrast them to other women in the world.

I began by defining *la Chicana* as a Mexican-American female who has minority status in her own land even though she is, in part, indigenous to the Americas and a member of one of the largest (majority) ethnic groups in the United States. She is a woman whose life is too often characterized by poverty, racism, and sexism not only in the dominant culture, but also within her own culture. Rarely do public officials or scholars perceive how this is so within a complex network of social forces; nor is she perceived as a woman who struggles to overcome the barriers of racism and sexism. Little attention has been given to her power, her cultural achievements, her successes, and her social rewards. Chicanas are also not characterized as members of a conquering and conquered culture rooted in the Spanish language, but married to Indian society. These women are part Indian and are contemporary women often lumped together with other U.S. Latinas (Puerto Rican, Cuban, Central and South American women) as if there were no diversity among these women. Their historical origin can be traced to the oldest Indian and European settlers in the Southern and Northern Hemisphere. These women are also U.S. citizens with full legal rights and responsibilities for whom there is unofficial discrimination. Because more often than not, they resemble other Latinas, it is difficult to distinguish them from undocumented women in the United States, and they very often get treated

This Chinese woman enjoyed having her picture taken. Photograph by Sandra Romero.

like undocumented, or newly arrived, Latino immigrants. Frequently, this treatment is negative.

The U.S. Latina shares the same male-dominated history as other Latina women. In 1502, Columbus encountered indigenous people living in Nicaragua. The Spaniards explored the Americas interacting with indigenous people and produced the mixed-blood mestizo that also represents the Chicano people who live in the United States. As in other countries, Chicanos experienced a succession of explorations, settlements, and revolutions that resulted in the United States' occupation of Mexico. Chicanos, like some Puerto Ricans, for example, want independence of U.S. occupation because they believe colonialism characterizes the relationship between themselves and the United States. Most Chicanos feel it is best to remain U.S. citizens and to struggle for civil rights. Only a very few still yearn for independence. Like some Puerto Ricans, some Chicanos feel that the current governing condition is a form of autonomy, their membership being in one of the strongest nations in the world. They sacrifice culture. Critics of this perspective believe that this is a political state of purgatory, or never-never land, with second-class citizenship. Those seeking independence want liberation from a colonial power and seek first class citizenship. Chicanas and Puerto Rican women have the legal right to move on and off of the mainland, and to have U.S. currency. Puerto Rican women rank just above Chicanas in their labor market participation rates. Both women have low labor market standing and low education, and tend to be poor. Many Puerto Rican women are single-parent heads of households. Some Chicanas share this condition, but most tend to be married. Puerto Ricans, however, are island people who migrated to the mainland United States. In contrast, Chicanas developed on the mainland.

Even though Puerto Ricans have had a strong presence on the mainland since the nineteenth century, the older women tended to immigrate after World War II, especially between 1950 and 1960. They tended to follow men who were attracted by the U.S. need for cheap labor on the east coast and by the collapse of the sugar plantation system. This pattern of following men for economic reasons is shared by Mexican and other women who immigrate to the United States from other parts of the Americas. Prior to the 1980s, earlier migration patterns included males settling in the host country. They then brought wives and families. More recently, entire or parts of families have been migrating together. While Puerto Ricans tended to settle in the Bronx and Brooklyn in New York and in Chicago, where there were networks, or at least a nucleus, of other Puerto Ricans, Latinos from other countries generally concentrated in the Southwest.

With regard to color, some Latinas are white, others high yellow, and still others black. In the 1970s the Chicano civil rights movement established the term *Chicano* and a radical political framework of thought that encouraged social criticism and pride in the historical and cultural past, promoted self-dignity, and affirmed the uniqueness of this identity (Gomez-Quinones, 1990). Defining la Chicana is complex because not all Chicanas are Mexican American and not all Mexican Americans self-identify as Chicanas. Self-identification is important because it is a matter of social consciousness that generally defines how these women conceptualize themselves. Some of the different labels (Hispanic, Latino, or country of origin) by which the group identifies itself have been reviewed in the Introduction. Naturally, there is a resistance to official definitions that have been imposed by the dominant culture. More germane to the discussion of identity are the historical facts that Chicana ancestors were first under Spanish rule and then were ruled by the French government before they interacted with the United States. In 1848, they became U.S. citizens, and in the 1960s, they adopted the label *Chicano*. But they have also been called Spanish surnamed, Mexican Americans, Hispanics, and Latinos.

Chicanas are a racial group, half Indian, half Spanish; and they are ethnic, practicing in a distinct culture. They are members of a conquering race dominated by males, and they are Indian women who provided services for their conquerors. They are products of violence and rape. Thus, they appear to be a product of contradiction. They sort through all labels, categories, their contradictory history, and their oppression, and then mix it and squeeze it through a psychic sieve, gathering the strands at the other end to continue to exist. This makes them strong, knowing there is no mechanism in the dominant society by which to adequately self-identify. They emerge whole, redefining themselves in response to historical circumstance, and they retain their power through fortitude, and perseverance. They have learned when to fight and when to retreat, when to engage in electoral politics and when to concentrate on nonelectoral matters. They know that colonization is a powerful force, demanding powerful reactions. That Chicanas remain on earth is a tribute to their persistence and social engineering.

In defining a feminist consciousness, the Chicana must wonder how much she has internalized sexism and how feminine she is when she is not the dominant model of femininity. She wonders how to be accepted to "American" culture and how close to white her skin color can get. Some will be happy to tell her; they do in many ways through the media, textbooks, teachers, and so on. She has to decide how to balance the mental burden to create and produce original art, music, food, and poetry. If she identifies herself economically, she quickly learns there is something missing. That something is her indigenous center, that thing that stabilizes human beings, that keeps them rooted wherever they go. It is that sense of spirituality that one is whole, like the curandera's (healer's) special healing power, the bruja's (sorceress' or witch's) power to bewitch, the sacred virgin's (Virgin Mary's) gentleness. This power is scary like that of la llorona, who drowned her children. That she can be all these and do so much is an extraordinary feat, providing miraculous answers to the mysteries of being human.

Yet she is the woman attached to the Spanish conquistador as daughter, wife, and mother. She was a product of those who brought private property, Christianity, and patriarchy in the form that we understand it today. What we witness when we are in her presence took over 500 years to create. Thus, not all women have grown in the same ideological direction at the same time. Therefore, there are Chicanas who know nothing about indigenous heritage or their spiritual power because of internalized discrimination; they do not want to be identified with the term *Chicana* because it has nationalist and radical connotations. More than anything, these women want to increase their social distance from anything that is politically and culturally Latino.

The term *Chicana* has feminist (political) overtones but also denotes the feminine gender. Some women do not want to be identified with it because they think feminism is linked to male bashing or to lesbianism. Much education has to be done here, but much education is also needed in defining Chicanas, who have also been referred to as Spanish, Mexican, Hispanic, Chicano, and Latino females. Latino has to do with the Latin base of the Spanish language. The word *Chicano* is rooted in the Chicano civil rights movement of the 1960s and is a political, ideological term, describing a group of people with shared cultural variables and political interpretations of their experiences. Because some women who are not Mexican American, but are Latinas, understand this experience, and because they have had similar experiences, they also call themselves Chicanas. In fact, the term *Chicana*, like *Chicano*, is a self-selected term that identifies women with a challenging ideology with regard to racism and sexism. Basically, the term *Chicana* implies some understanding of the history of the neglect, double standard, and discrimination endured by Mexican Americans and other Latino people in the United States. Those with this understanding adopt lifestyles that frequently lead them to advocate on behalf of their people.

Chicano and Latino people have been categorized as one unit primarily by the Anglo-dominated culture for the sake of convenience; the Anglos do not understand the diversity of the Spanish-speaking language. The term *Hispanic* defines persons of Spanish-language culture, and may include Central and Latin Americans, persons from Cuba and Puerto Rico, Spanish Europeans, and Chicanos. Latino also refers to all of the above-mentioned groups but excludes Spanish Europeans. Generally, Chicanos and Chicanas are labeled nationalist, civil rights activists, or grassroots organizers. As mentioned, they have also been called Hispanics, and not all Hispanics or Latinos relate positively to activism. Chicanas may call themselves Chicano when relating generically to the group, regardless of gender. In this text, the words *Mexican American, Mexicana, Chicana, Hispanic*, and *Latina* are frequently used, and an attempt has been made to keep the meaning consistent with the definitions outlined above. The reader should be aware that other scholars often use the terms interchangeably.

REFERENCES

Associated Press. 1990. *China: From the Long March to Tiananmen Square*. New York: Henry Holt and Co.

Fisher, Maxine P. 1989. *Women in the Third World*. New York: Franklin Watts.

Gomez-Quinones, Juan. 1990. *Chicano Politics: Reality and Promise, 1940–1990*. Albuquerque: University of New Mexico Press.

United Nations Department of Public Information. 1985. "World Survey on the Role of Women in Development." Report. Recorded in *Review and Appraisal*. New York.

U.S. Department of Commerce, Economics and Statistics Administration, Bureau of the Census. 1993. *We the American . . . Foreign Born*. Washington, D.C.: Government Printing Office.

———. 1993. *We the American Hispanics*. Washington, D.C.: Government Printing Office.

2

STRUGGLING TO PARTICIPATE

As stated in Chapter 1, U.S. Latinas had difficulty attending the first international conference on women in Mexico City for three reasons: racism, access to information, and economics. In terms of access to information, Chicanas were the most likely to find out about the conference because of their involvement with nongovernmental agencies and because of their community advocacy work. When news of the U.N. conference began to circulate, few Chicanas ventured into primarily white women's network to inquire what was taking place, why it was taking place, when the conference would be held, and how to participate. In the 1970s Mexican-American women in the United States did not interact with white women on an equal footing. In many respects, this remains true today. Racial animosity, hatred, and historical traditions prevent white women and women of color from truly interacting, much less participating in a joint effort. Thus, in the mid-1970s, the struggle in the United States was over who would be a delegate to the conference.

GAINING KNOWLEDGE

Chicanas were at a severe disadvantage. There were too many things they did not know. For one thing, most Chicanas had no idea what a delegate was and how the delegates were to be chosen. Some found out that to be a delegate meant that the airfare and the hotel expenses for

Latinas struggle to arrive at the NGO Conference. Photograph by Sandra Romero.

the trip would be provided. They wanted to attend the discussion on women, but they did not understand that one objective of the conference was to draw up a plan of action for the protection of women's rights and to present it to the United Nations for ratification sometime in the future.

Only a few years before the 1975 conference, the United States had undergone what some social scientists and governmental officials feared could become a social revolution. Youth, among them Chicana and Chicano youth, revolted against socially prescribed class, racial, ethnic, age, and gender norms that they found much too limiting. Various forms of civil rights protests were launched: the black civil rights movement, the Hippie movement, the women's movement, the antiwar movement, the American Indian movement, and the Chicano movement. The feared social revolution did not in the end come about because those involved in the movement had not dealt effectively with their classism and racism. These were the goals of some persons in the various movements, but the movements were infiltrated by entities seeking to fragment them. Moreover the social realities of classism and racism were too firmly ingrained in the dominant ideology.

At the height of social criticism in the United States, Anglo feminists controlled the white feminist movement, and their issues were at the forefront. With some effort, Chicanas could relate well to most of these concerns, but they saw women's lives through their own experience. They experienced sexism within their own culture, their own movement, their own families, and the larger communities. But in the larger society they also experienced racism from both white men and white women. Some early white feminist concerns included the need for more challenging lives and greater intimacy with their male counterparts. This makes sense if one is a middle-class white woman whose husband is on an upwardly mobile track. But Chicanas were poor, and needed relief from poverty. Thus, in the very beginning, they had little in common with white women. When the issues of equal pay for equal work and the right of women to control their own bodies through access to birth control and abortion became a priority for white women in the 1960s, Chicanas began to pay more attention to the white feminist movement because this was within the realm of their experience.

Control of reproduction became as important an issue as equal pay for equal work. For Chicanas it was not so much that too many children caused poverty; rather, it was that childbirth was so very hard on their minds and their bodies. At that time, the average married Chicana had five or six children. Most doctors were white and insensitive to Chicana cultural needs; and because the Chicano population was mostly Catholic, then, as now, the Vatican prohibited birth control. Thus, the issue of birth control became heavily linked to reforming the Catholic Church. Most white feminists were Protestant, and while reforming the church was important, it was not the leading priority. The priority, rather, was upward mobility. While poverty was the Chicana's driving concern, it was nowhere near the top of the list for white feminists. Their sense of upward mobility was moving up within the middle and upper class. Chicanas were therefore greatly mistaken when they thought they would get support for their issues from the mostly white feminists, who wanted representation in even higher levels of employment, education, politics, and decision making. Chicanas and Chicanos had little or no access to these entities.

White women did not make any connection between racism and gender discrimination, and did not see Chicanas as females and people of color at the same time. Unable to split themselves into two and to make the choice that white women told them they had to make, the Chicanos had to choose between the feminist movement and the Chicano movement. The request that they make such a choice was insulting. It was politically, socially, physically, and spiritually impossible to choose between being female and being a person of color. Chicanas and other women of color would not and could not choose. They proceeded to address their own concerns and the concerns of their people within the context of their own nationalist movements. Some remained in the struggle in order to persuade these movements to hear and understand Chicanas; most did not. The entire ordeal helped fragment the women's movement in the United States.

Chicanas and other "minority women" struggled to take part in the feminist movement until the first world women's conference in Mexico City. By the time delegates to the Mexico City conference were to be selected, it had become crystal clear that the division was too deep. Bitter fights were fought, and Chicanas were underrepresented, if represented at all. It was at about this time that Chicanas began to be referred to as "Third World women" in the United States, implying that they were disempowered women. They were vindicated, however, when Mexican women and other "Third World women" from underdeveloped countries confronted U.S. women in Mexico City. The U.S. women were told that they were patronizing, arrogant, and opportunistic, and that they would have to share the agenda with women of color from other parts of the world. As a result of this confrontation, I organized the First Colorado Chicana Conference in Boulder, Colorado, in 1977, and other Chicana conferences were held in other parts of the Southwest.

THE MEXICO—U.S. BORDER

The border between Mexico and the United States is more than an international demarcation. It is symbolic of what separates the developed from the underdeveloped world, that line which when crossed changes lives. It is for this change in life chances that multitudes from all over the Americas are drawn to the border. That invisible serpentine line drawn by powerful hands along the Rio Grande both divides and unites two very different worlds (Dale and Sartore, 1996). There, one finds two economies—remnants of the Old West, faith and folk healers, shopping, riches and poverty, garment workers, prostitutes, nightclub owners, animal racing, a yearning for technology and women in search of a coyote (someone to bring them across the border into the United States). Most U.S. Latinas tend to come from the northern, poorest regions of Mexico, but they represent all parts and classes of Mexico and Central and South America, especially Guatemala, Nicaragua, El Salvador, Peru, Ecuador, and Chile. Some of the women are indigenous, originating in El Salvador and Guatemala. They speak regional dialects as a first language, and they speak Spanish knowing they will have to learn English.

In one study of immigrant women in a course I taught at California State University in Los Angeles, I and the class interviewed roughly forty women. The study focused on the forces motivating migration, women's expectations, migration and the americanization experience, and their assessment of the process. Women were interviewed both individually and in clusters using an interview guide. Because of their undocumented status, it was difficult to sample these women. Most were friends of friends. In the main, they were severely intimidated by nonimmigrants, especially researchers, whom they perceived as reeking of U.S. government ties, especially la migra, the U.S. immigration officials. To the inexperienced eye, all immigrant Latinas may look the same, but they differ not only in their appearance, but also in how they speak Spanish, the length of time they tend to be in the states, their degree of fluency in English, the ways they conduct their daily affairs, their sense of space, and their spirituality. Some subjects of the study had higher education and owned their own businesses. Also among them were professional women and homemakers, street vendors, prostitutes, and even drug addicts. They varied in a multitude of areas and were, in fact, quite diverse.

The Latinas immigrated as children, teenagers, young adults, middle-aged adults, and senior citizens. Many immigrated without family. Some women came to join their husbands, who were already in southern California. Others came with children, and many without them. Some brought one or two children and left others behind hoping to earn enough money to send for them. These women risked much to travel a few blocks or thousands of miles on foot. They also used public transportation, including air transportation. They arrived in the United States using all modes of travel available and in any combination.

A few patterns emerged from this study. This pilot study set the groundwork for more extensive research. What it did uncover was that women who immigrate are taken advantage of, even exploited. When they finally arrive in the United States, they usually are taken in by relatives or friends. Making money becomes the next challenge. Most work as domestics. Those who come with children have an extra burden beyond clothing, food, and shelter: they must also enroll the child in school.

A few women reported that living in the United States was great from the time of their arrival. Generally, they said that during the first three to six years they missed many things from their country, not just the people and the sights and sounds, but also the flowers and the fauna. Nonetheless, they were glad to have the opportunity to be in the states. What they liked best was the idea of democracy. Although many had fled from political oppression, most came for economic reasons. The poverty from which they had escaped was more than economic; it also included their country's woefully inadequate health services and education. After their children entered school, the children learned the course material and made the transition to English-speaking teachers. Most parents pressured children not to get behind in their studies while learning the language. The pressure was motivated by their desire for a better life for their children than they had. They deprived themselves a lot on behalf of the children. Parents with teenagers had special needs, for as is true of any teens, they needed to fit in with their peers and break away from being a child to become a young adult. Of course, gaps developed between parents and children. Those who immigrated as teens frequently learned English faster than their parents and became the parents' and grandparents' translators. Sometimes this situation provoked a power struggle between adult and offspring. If the offspring learned to drive or had access to a vehicle, they would take the parents to obtain services and to purchase food. Most women walked to buy food. Some even sold food from carts and in restaurants.

Since this project sought to identify patterns of social perception and general behavior, it was especially interested in the immigrant Latina experience with U.S.-born Chicanas. Most women found Chicanas very interesting. They did not see them as their most immediate frame of reference. Sometimes they viewed Chicanas with some degree of misunderstanding and envy. Many immigrant Latinas reported being treated very well by the Chicanas. Chicanas frequently were a source of information, which is so important to all new arrivals, but some Chicanas treated them with hostility, laughing at them for being *mojados*, (''wetbacks''). Most Chicanas wanted to know what the immigrant was ''doing here,'' making it clear (sometimes with hostility, sometimes with sincere innocence) that they were insiders and that the immigrant was an outsider. The immigrant Latinas reported experiencing some meanness on the streets. All but two reported being laughed at, demeaned, or demoralized. Many teens guiltily admitted being ashamed of their parents.

Our class study showed that U.S. Latinas are categorized by residential status, which may cause problems in fostering a more united women's movement. Before we move too quickly to this conclusion, however, the dichotomy is something that most Latinas do not fully recognize. Once creating unity between the groups becomes an issue, it can be easily resolved. The problem now is that Latinas do not understand one another at the personal level. Although they have some abstract understanding of the immigration process, few have discussed perceptions of one another and the idea of unifying as a Latina interest group. The ultimate form of female liberation is that of enlightenment, which leads to defining and redefining until the need no longer exists. Latinas do not have a finely structured feminist ideology because they are a highly diverse group of women. In fact, a few Chicanas have been defining the feminist perspective for many women.

CHALLENGING THE THIRD WORLD CONCEPT

Chicanas and Latinas are frequently lumped together into a Third World perspective. The phrase "Third World" can be traced to the explosion of the hydrogen bomb in Japan at the end of World War II. This event changed the world forever. It established the United States as the most feared nation and created an international hierarchical structure that constructed the "Third World." Contemporary women have been trying to keep the nation from war in order to protect human civilization ever since. In order to do this better, the world must be redefined. The fact that most of the world is populated by people of color from underdeveloped countries makes them the majority.

The concept of the "Third World" is used primarily by hierarchically thinking, male, politicians, journalists, and scholars to refer to those countries that have been in powerless positions and unable to align themselves politically with either the United States or the old structure of the Soviet Union. Maxine P. Fisher (1989) lends support to this definition and observes that the United Nations does not use the term, preferring instead the term *developing countries*. Developing countries, lacking resources and political alliance, suffer from human inability to respond to environmental hardships. Paul Harrison (1981) gives us some insights into this matter in his discussion of geographical regions that experience long periods of drought or rainfall. However, he writes about weather patterns as extremes, independent of the human ability to respond based on political, economic, and educational power. This translates into technology and the ability to acquire substantial outside support from other countries to meet the hardships endured by people who whether by luck, accident, or destiny were born in harsh climates/ or were forced to live there.

Harrison writes about the injustice of nature and the injustice of man. The reader is asked to note that nature is feminine and that what she delivers is part of the life cycle. Most people from developing countries do not have the insatiable need to impose their will on nature, thereby upsetting the life cycle. According to Harrison, poverty contributes both to the cause and the impact of disaster. It is a major cause of deforestation (cutting down the forest) and desertification (destroying the desert), both of which aggravate floods and droughts. People from developing countries view the "Third World" as being based on the greed of the already rich, most of whom are white males trading and selling in the world market. It is this greed that causes poverty. As the Chicanos understand, poor people are forced to participate in their own underdevelopment by the gluttonous appetite of the rich male for profit. The Chicanas have seen it happen to their own people, on their own land. A foreign white people moved in, took control and maintained control using violence, appropriated the land and its resources, and entrapped the population into the role of cheap laborers, relegating women to the home, and they also imposed their religion, ideology, and way of life. Chicanas have taken a vow of resistance to this occupation. Resistance is in the form of dressing, talking, voting, insisting on indigenous spirituality, eliminating violence, returning to a healthy environment, which includes respect for the land, access to resources, relief from poverty, and establishing alternative ways of thinking and doing things in their country.

Chicanas and Latinas should not adopt this Third World position, for to do so places them in a hierarchy of class and color. In the world, most women in the global women's movement are women of color, and therefore are the majority. Chicanas and Latinas should challenge white women in setting the women's agenda in the United States, for there they also are the majority. In addition, the global agenda needs to be thrust to the forefront in the United States. Since the United States has many unresolved problems with racism, elimination of racism at any cost, especially in the women's movement, must be a priority.

THE CHICANA CIVIL RIGHTS MOVEMENT

The 1960s, gave birth to the civil rights movement in the United States. Chicana feminists persisted in drawing attention to what white women then called minority female concerns. Chicanas noted that sexism, like racism, functioned to the disadvantage of all women in a class society. These were loud, angry, hostile times that encompassed not only the Hippie and the women's movements, but also anti-Vietnam War protests, relaxed standards in hair and dress styles, free sex, rock music, and drugs. In the Chicano movement, there were strikes, boycotts, and marches protesting the treatment of grape and lettuce harvesters. Led by Cesar Chavez, the Chicanos urged the nation not to make purchases at stores that carried these targeted foods. During this time, educational demonstrations were staged demanding Chicano Studies on university and college campuses, a lower dropout rate, better teachers, improved facilities, and a more relevant curriculum. The demand for Chicana Studies came after women became involved in the movement and realized that men took advantage of their hard work in their own name. In the early stages of the development of Chicano Studies, marches, sit-ins, and pickets were held. A few Chicano Hippies sang love and peace songs and wore flowers in their hair, but most wore sarapes, head bands, and Emiliano Zapata or Che Guevera t-shirts.

During this time Chicanas joined youth groups such as Movimiento Estudiantil Chicano de Aztlan (MECHA), the United Mexican American Students (UMAS), and the Brown Berets. Many Chicano men entered serious relationships or had sex with Anglo females for the first time; some married them. As a result, discussions of the "white goddess" syndrome came to the forefront. Sexual politics was a heated discussion whenever Chicanas pointed out that even Chicanos had internalized the notion that white women were the standard of beauty, the prized possession. Anglo men rarely went with Chicanas; but when it happened, Chicanas were harassed and called "sellouts." In the 1960s, white men and women, Native Americans, blacks, Chicanos and Chicanas, and Asians all wanted a different society. On some issues they agreed; on the gender issue they did not.

Some of today's more youthful activists long for heated debate on most social arrangements. Those who experienced it in the 1960s lament that they had great dreams but did not accomplish as much as they desired. On the contrary, they accomplished a great deal. Chicanos claimed their homeland and called it Aztlan (Anaya and Lomeli, 1991), and they made the world of U.S. Latinas just a little better by breaking away from traditional approaches to women's roles. They were visible and for the first time they addressed the issues of self-concept, identity, self-determination, and political action (Gomez-Quinones, 1990). Some Chicanos wanted a revolution. They proclaimed that they should take up arms, have Aztlan secede from the nation, and rule themselves free from racism. Others thought the movement should proceed with much more caution, avoiding violence. During this crucial era, both Chicanas and Chicanos participated in the nationwide Chicano Moratorium protesting the war in Vietnam, in which a disproportionate number of Chicano young men were being killed. A major riot broke out on August 29, 1970 in Los Angeles. In Denver there was a major "walkout" of public schools in protest both of a curriculum that excluded the Chicano story and culturally biased and unjust academic standards. The very few women who demanded that Chicano Studies also include Chicanas encountered resistance from both men and women.

Chicanas wore blue jeans. Chicano parents hated this symbol of a working man on their daughters. Women were not considered workers, even though they worked long hours in the home. Both males and females put on t-shirts not because they were the latest fashion, but because they also represented what the working-class male wore. When Chicana mothers commented that t-shirts displayed too much of the girls' breasts, some took off both t-shirt and bra, and instead wore halter tops. The focus for these Chicanas was racism, class discrimination, and gender bias. They demanded a better quality of life for women, less restricted roles, and greater representation in all elements of the government and the Chicano movement. Some Chicanas experimented with drugs and sex in ways their mothers would never have imagined, and there was little discussion between such mothers and daughters. In fact, most Chicanas deliberately limited times with their mothers, and when they were together, Chicanas rarely spoke about what they were doing. *Vergüenza* (shame) was the element involved here; but it was more than this. The mother could not, indeed would not, understand; and out of respect and the desire not to prolong the conflict, Chicanas were not going to disclose much of their lifestyle. Besides, they were also involved in a struggle with their male counterparts. Fighting arose over what being a "good girl," a good Catholic, a good citizen, and a good Chicana were about. Some young women were "kicked" out of their homes. Many of them went to the university and eventually became elementary school principals, professors, and elected politicians. At no other time were Mexican-American young women more active and visible on the streets, in the schools, in the media, in the parks, everywhere in the Southwest. But with no economic and material resources, reform won out over revolution.

When feminist rhetoric gradually was translated into action, lower class women and women of color rarely become empowered by the feminist movement. Great gaps still remain between white women and women of color in terms of quality of life, upward mobility, political representation, health, education, and the criminal justice system. Leading Chicana feminists still remember the fact that the feminist movement was closed to Chicanas in the United States. White women had a patronizing attitude toward Chicanas; and the tendency is still to see race relations as a black/white phenomenon. Women of color get lost in the hierarchical dichotomy of color in the United States.

By the late 1970s women of color, especially Chicanas, had tired of the white feminists' inability to deal effectively with their racism and classism. Chicanas were not deeply interested in lesbian issues or the political ideologies that fragmented that movement. They abandoned the white-dominated, predominantly middle-class women's movement for their own feminist movement within their nationalism movement, and proceeded simultaneously. This movement addressed the privilege of patriarchy and demanded representation and participation in all movement decisions. Male resistance escalated, but there was no returning to old relationships, and Chicanas still conceived of themselves as "minority women" in the 1970s.

Most Chicanas, like black women, never abandoned their men and their people while striving to gain equal rights for women. When black and Chicano women compared notes with one another, they discovered that they were having the same experiences with both the Anglo feminists and their civil rights movement. Black women were reacting to the white feminist movement in much the same way as the Chicanas had. These "minority" women formed the first coalitions at meetings and conferences where white women were involved. In these coalitions, they developed an ideology that strengthened the women of color movement. In the late 1970s, some Anglo feminists were trying to deal effectively with their own racism, but little had been resolved. These women tended to be white socialist and communist women, who advocated the overthrow of capitalism and the construction of an entirely different social structure. Chicanas were not sure they wanted to support this radical plank; they wanted to share in the leadership of any discussions. Liberal white women were not going to let this happen. On the surface, this appeared to be a good alliance but white socialist and communist feminism had another hidden agenda. They were recruiting for their own parties. Chicanas did not join either party in any great numbers.

WOMEN OF COLOR GO TO BEIJING

It was not until about the 1980s that white women and Chicanas began to call themselves "Third World women." The 1980s was declared the decade of the Hispanic and the U.N. Decade for Women. Both declarations spurred a lot of talk. The decade of the Hispanic replaced the word *Chicano* in most conversation, which tended to focus on the rapidly rising demographic profile of the population and its potential as a voting bloc. For women the talk revolved around sexual segregation, unequal allotment of government funding, stereotypes in books and other media, and educational content. Most Chicanas were not aware that the United Nations had declared 1975 to 1985 the U.N. Decade for Women. It was in the late 1980s that Chicanas began to see the elitism of the term *Third World* (Blea, 1990) and how it relegated them to a lower status.

In the 1990s, Chicanas accepted the label "women of color" as a way to get others to deal with the reality of color stratification in U.S. society.

During the first part of the decade, they experimented with an X spelling of the word Chicana, Xicana. Nonprogressive male scholars resisted the Mexica (Aztec) and Spanish origin of the *ch* sound as symbolic of the Spanish oppression of indigenous people in Mexico, especially the women. Most women did not pay attention to the eurocentic linguistic interpretation and saw the effort as male pressure to get them to back away from continuing to self-define.

In 1996, U.S. women of color formed a coalition whose goal was to have the U.N. platform on women's rights include a statement that feminized racism. Just as poverty became a feminist issue, so women of color were successful in getting into the international document the idea that most women in the world are women of color and have endured the racism of white dominated countries via war and economic and political exploitation. The effort began in 1975 in Mexico City, and it took thirty years to accomplish. U.S. women of color went to Beijing to participate in a gathering of nations in order to get to know other women like themselves, to discuss the problems of women of color, to identify women they could work with, to redefine human rights as women's rights, to explore transforming institutions to become more sensitive to women's needs, and to create a document on the specific needs of women for the United Nations. This document is to be ratified by all U.N. nations and implemented as national policy among member nations of the United Nations.

Mine was apparently the only presentation on Chicanas on the official NGO program. The one and one-half hour presentation consisted of both lecture and reading of my original poetry. My session was well attended by women of the United States, a male from Great Britain, two Asian women, three African women, and roughly eleven Chicanas who were surprised to see one another. Most persons in the tent that housed the presentation were not aware of the celebration taking place within each Chicana present. It was not until we got a chance to talk, after the session, that we noted that the celebration was finally getting international attention. Meanwhile, during the presentation, a thorough, civil, highly intellectual, yet basic discussion was held on the issues of U.S. Chicanas. Chicanas and Latinas are very adept at presenting both a private and a public face—and at knowing when to show which.

REFERENCES

Anaya, Rudolfo A., and Francisco A. Lomeli, eds. 1991. *Aztlan: Essays on the Chicano Homeland*. Albuquerque: University of New Mexico Press.

Blea, Irene I. 1990. *La Chicana and the Intersection of Race, Class and Gender*. New York: Praeger.

Castillo, Ana. 1995. *Massacre of the Dreamers: Essays on Xicanisma*. Albuquerque: University of New Mexico Press.

Dale, Bruce, and Joel Sartore. 1996, February. "Tex Mex Border." *National Geographic*, pp. 44–69.

Fisher, Maxine P. 1989. *Women in the Third World*. New York: Franklin Watts.

Gomez-Quinones, Juan. 1990. *Chicano Politics: Reality and Promise, 1940–1990*. Albuquerque: University of New Mexico Press.

Harrison, Paul. 1981. *Inside the Third World*. New York: Penguin Books.

3

DEFINING CHICANA FEMINISM

While many U.S. Latinas are immigrants, Chicanas tend not to be. They are mostly American-born citizens who have both indigenous and Spanish European ancestry. They are very interested in immigration because most other Americans cannot distinguish between foreign-born Latinas and Chicanas, and because immigration policy affects Chicanas when they are subject to immigrant bashing and discrimination.

During the preparation for the 1995 Beijing conference, I would define the origin and meaning of Chicana by giving the definition presented in the introduction of this text. The most commonly asked question was, Where does the word *Chicana* come from? The broadly accepted origin of the word is in the word Mexica (Aztec), where the *x* is pronounced *sh*. The Mexican became known as the Mexicano, and Chicano simply evolved from the dropping of *M* and *e*, and converting the *sh* sound to *ch*. An extension of the definition requires a focus on the social, physical, psychological, and spiritual definition of Chicanas within the social-historical context of the United States.

SOCIAL AND HISTORICAL CONTEXT

As is true of the Chinese in particular, ancestry plays an important role in the lives of Chicanas. It places them in a social-historical context recognized each year in the commemoration of the ancestors in *el Día de*

The women at the Beijing and Huairou conferences were closely watched by the Chinese government. The surveillance eased after the women complained loudly. Photograph by Sandra Romero.

los Muertos (the Day of the Dead). Chicanas are also strongly influenced by the memory of the nineteenth-century U.S. war with Mexico, whose culmination resulted in their ancestors becoming U.S. citizens. It influenced the definition of Chicana by placing her in a position subordinate to the male ancestors who lost the war and who were further victimized because the United States did not honor the provisions of the international treaty known as the Treaty of Guadalupe Hidalgo signed in 1848. In fact, the definition of la Chicana revolves around labeling and resisting the labels and stereotypes rooted in reactions to this war experience. Perhaps there are some advantages to using labels, but in the cases involving race relations, generally there are disadvantages to those being defined. The disadvantaged can be summarized in the stereotypes emanating from the period around 1848: Chicanas are lazy, unclean, and sexually available.

Many U.S. Latinas are indigenous people to the Americas who intermarried with the Spanish conqueror to produce a new race, the mestizo. Most early Chicana ancestors entered what is now known as the U.S. Southwest by traveling along the Camino Real (the Royal Road) in carts and on horses, but not before making their way across the vast territory of Mexico, conquering the mighty Mexica, fighting and intermarrying with other indigenous tribes. Because the Spanish won the wars, they (like the Americans when they won the U.S. war with Mexico) got to write the history and they excluded the history of the conquered. This is why we know more about the Spanish than we do about the indigenous, especially the women, who taught the Spanish much about how to live in the territory. The indigenous had a key role in developing the Spanish plan for the vast region. They built missions, enhanced the art and music, taught the healing capabilities of herbs, tended livestock, assisted in food cultivation and storage, constructed clothing, and provided a variety of services and free labor.

Generally, the term *Chicana* has feminist and nationalistic connotations, and therefore, political overtones. Most Latinas do not have the same understanding of how the U.S. social structure functions to displace Chicanas. Therefore, they do not always share the same ideology and insistence on using the term *Chicana*. In the past, Chicanas have been referred to as Spanish, Spanish-speaking, Mexican, Mexican-American, Hispanic, Chicano, and Latino females. The most recently applied label is the term *Latina*. There are bad words, racist and sexist words, like mamasita (little hot mama) and hot tamale, used to describe Chicanas. Chicana feminists have dealt with these words for over one hundred fifty years. They have been stereotyped as bitches, lesbians, man haters, ball busters, and other much less flattering names. More than anything else, *Chicana* is a term describing a group of women with shared cultural values and shared political interpretations of their experience in the United States. This is coupled with a lifestyle that advocates on behalf of women and Latino people via civil rights activism. They may be lower class, grassroots organizers, middle and upper class; or women with higher education or very little education. They may even call themselves Hispanic, but not all Hispanics advocate empowering raza (Chicano/Latino people), much less raza women.

Images of la Chicana range from the fat, abnegated, passive woman to the sensuous Hollywood spitfire. The fat Chicana is a good cook, loves her children, but is too ignorant to know how to discipline them. She is also so needy that she puts up with an unfaithful, and frequently drunk, husband, who has children with other women. This image of men is not flattering, and men have a lot of work to do in this department. Nevertheless, Chicanas struggle to address Hollywood vamp images which challenge the puritan Anglo woman image for the favors of the Anglo leading man, who is the prize. The Mexican "señorita" is often characterized as jealous and possessing only her sexuality as bait for him. In contrast, the Anglo woman is pure, intelligent, and dignified. The Anglo male, symbolized by the American cowboy, has a sexual liaison with the Mexican prostitute but marries the white woman, settles down, and raises beautiful blond, blue-eyed children, preferably male children.

In her own culture, la Chicana images range from sainted mother to that of an evil witch who entraps men into falling in love with her. She is either property or wild, horrifying, and untamed, like la llorona, the wailing witchlike female in search of the souls of her children. Women are to be feared and avoided, punished and controlled, engaged as virgins, confined in marriage, isolated for male use only. Male children learn to exclude their mothers from these images. Only other women are this way. Female children grow up fearing the stereotypes and strive to be like their mother, whose role model is La Virgen de Guadalupe, the bronze indigenous and European saint representing the mother of Jesus Christ.

The problem with any stereotype is that there is sometimes a little bit of truth in it. This tiny grain of truth is amplified, twisted to fit the dominant image of women, especially Mexican women, and used to the male advantage. If Chicanas are jealous, they are jealous for the same reason other women are jealous—they have been made to feel insecure. This insecurity is rooted in male patriarchy, where men hold the most valued social position and entertain themselves in female competition. Because white men have needed to control the elements of competition, which leads to profit, they have discriminated against white women and all people of color. What most do not recognize is that, contrary to popular stereotype, Chicano culture has not always been as male dominated as some would like to believe. One should not surmise, however, that it is matriarchal. Research (Baca-Zinn 1975a, 1975b; Veyna, 1986; and

Ybarra 1977, 1982a, 1982b) suggests that perhaps intimate Chicano culture is more egalitarian than the dominant Anglo culture. It is my contention that as Chicanos (males) become more urbanized, more Americanized, and more disempowered, the status of women becomes lower.

The use of language is important to Chicanas. Generally, Chicanas speak Spanish but not always. Many are monolingual English but practice Chicano culture. Most things in the Spanish language have gender, "o" ending words being male and "a" ending words female. Notably, there are more "o" ending words, and so the language is male dominant. The two most frequently used words in this book are Chicana and Latina. The reader should be informed that there is some resistance to the use of the word Latina. The root word "Latin" refers to persons of Greek origin and has nothing to do with persons from Spanish-language cultures. Latin, however, was the original language of the Catholic Church, and many believe the church has been oppressive to Latinos. Therefore, any reference to it, or to its mother language, is to be resisted. This leaves few choices, indicating that labeling has been dysfunctional. Arguments over what label to use have caused some fragmentation among Chicana feminists, leaving some important issues to go unaddressed. Persons are left with linguistic, emotional, and political wounds, which either take a long time to heal or do not heal at all.

Chicanos have few role models and even fewer mentors; thus, the consequences of deviating from prescribed roles can be devastating. The women who have successfully deviated from traditional roles have had to do so more or less alone. Their enemies have been both the visible and invisible forces of the intersecting variables of sexism and racism. Oppression requires unusual responses on behalf of the oppressed. The controlling forces of oppression, be they seen or unseen, are absorbing but can stimulate creativity and alternative thinking, learning and survival models. Creativity, for example, can be based on the need to survive. The Chicana has created some inspiring coping and living mechanisms.

ACADEMIC DEFINITION

Academic Chicana feminists have tended to define feminism for both Chicanas and Latinas. Most of the Chicanas who went to China in 1995 were more highly educated. But China had an impact on U.S. Chicanas long before the United Nations conference on women. Many Chicanas had studied Mao and the Chinese Communist Revolution in the 1970s as part of their participation in the Chicano movement. During this period, some advocated for social revolution, whereas others sought social reform in their own country. Some remnant of this study, especially the call for revolution, can still be found today in the more radical fundamental ideologies of Chicanas. I took this knowledge with me before traveling to China, when I attended study groups for six months on the subject of contemporary China. I was particularly interested in that period after its well-known social revolution. Mexico underwent a major revolution in 1910 that resulted in mass migration to the United States. Because the time I had available for reading was limited by all the requirements involved in writing my last book, *Researching Chicano Communities* (1995), and in fulfilling my teaching schedule and administrative duties as chairperson of the first Department of Chicano Studies in the nation, I turned to books on tape and videos, in addition to study groups. These readings included *Life and Death in Shanghai* by Nien Cheng (1987) and *Notes from China* by Barbara Wertheim Tuchman (1972). Cheng, an upper class Chinese citizen before the Chinese Revolution, renders her perspective on her experience during the Chinese Revolution. Tuchman was a five-week, middle-class, tourist who toured eleven Chinese cities with her daughter. For Valentine's Day my twenty-nine-year-old daughter gave me a very large book entitled *China: From the Long March to Tiananmen Square*, a collection of articles and photos gathered by the writers and photographers of the Associated Press from 1919 to 1989, when the student fervor rocked the Chinese government, culminating in the bloody massacre at Tiananmen Square. I also saw many feature-length films and documentaries, including *The Last Emperor*. While I was in China I picked up the autobiography of China's last emperor, Pu Yi, *From Emperor to Citizen: The Autobiography of Aisin-Gioro Pu Yi* (1989). In final preparation for my trip, I viewed the National Geographic film series entitled "The Silk Road."

I had been a life-long student of revolution and reform, and my career in working with scholars and students was full. As a student and a Chicano civil rights advocate, I had read that in China students had been at the forefront of every major upheaval in their country in the twentieth century. In my ongoing study of China, in some future text I hope to relate what we know about the civil unrest, revolution, reform, and role of students in China to the Chicano movement of the 1960s. When I went to China, I had a basic understanding of the Chinese, Russian and even the French revolutions. I had mostly studied the Mexican Revolution (1910–1917) and the role of women in that revolution, and so was deeply aware of my need for more insight into Chinese culture. Two of the books I had listened to were Nien Cheng's work (1987), and the one by Bette Boa Lord (1990), the Chinese wife of a former American ambassador to China. At this time, I was pleasantly surprised to receive a copy of *Chicano in China* by Rudolfo A. Anaya (1986), my novelist friend who had traveled to China ten years earlier. Anaya is also a well known literary figure with an interdisciplinary approach to the subject. He wrote his book after traveling to China. We both agreed that there are more similarities than differences between the Chinese and the Chicanos.

While more serious academic works had been written on the subject of modern-day China, I did not have time to explore them before my trip. Therefore, when I visited China, I was essentially a tourist, though with a social science background, I desired more from my trip than mere tourist information and vivid photographs. With regard to getting to know China, ultimately I was disappointed. I achieved a bit more than most tourists, but not much more. Thus my studies continue, just as my plans to return to do research on China's racial/ethnic minorities continue.

My emphasis on the social-historical context in Chicano Studies also continues. This context demands that scholars place the subject of research, inquiry, and discussion within the historical context of the development of the society in which it exists. In other words, the history must be explored but in an interdisciplinary manner. When studying and defining la Chicana, one must begin with indigenous women, the impact of Spanish male explorers on their land, cultural clashes and interchanges, the Anglo's impact on Spanish and Indian culture, and assimilation and acculturation into a highly hierarchical society. The researcher cannot assume that things are either all good or all bad. When engaged in study, the researcher must be detached but have a clear perspective on the subject. In the case of Chicanas, we must study how they perceive their own lives via an internal perspective grounded in their interpretation of their reality, as well as via an external perspective showing how their lives have been impacted by men, war, and governmental and societal changes. After having studied and written about the colonization of one culture by another, Chicano academics have rendered an academic perspective on their historical reality. This is why the U.S. war with Mexico, which ended in 1848 with the signing of the Treaty of Guadalupe Hidalgo, is so important. It was at this point that mestizo people were conquered and treated as strangers in their own land.

Definitions of women do not exist in either social or historical isolation of male deeds in time of war. Women are also defined by the land, the air, the water, their material culture, ancestors, spirituality, the political use of language, as well as the role of state and federal governments. They are defined by their social and historical conditions, by how they have been treated and how they treat one another, children, and the aged, by how they feel about what has happened, and by how they relate to what is happening to the next generation. Women inherit their societies, communities, and relatives when they are born. Thus, they inherit what has gone on before them. Some Chicanas grow up to live the life that is outlined for them. Some live and die quietly, while others grumble and complain. A few, however, rebel and struggle for change; it is they who leave a distinguished legacy.

The most recent major social change for the Chicanas came in the 1960s with the Chicano civil rights movement, when the movement women gave voice to their feminist perspective. Prior to this era, the most significant change had occurred for males during and after World War II, although this does not mean that women were not being introspective. It simply means that women's lives were not significantly documented before the 1960s. During the Chicano civil rights movement, communities began to host meetings at which historical, physical, and social living conditions were discussed. These gatherings produced nongovernmental organization and social action with regard to education, poverty, politics, housing, and feminism. Many Chicanas discovered that their leadership qualities could accomplish tasks outside the home and that they had power. Some even received local and national attention.

A historical review of that era reveals a highly male-dominant Chicano culture, although women had a large voice. The women's role is poorly documented because of the male-dominated media. Historians have for the most part been males interested in documenting male history using white male-dominated methodologies. But women were at the heart of the Chicano movement through their participation as organizers, boycotters, strikers, students, farm workers, clerical workers, fund raisers, and community outreach workers. They were present in the true communal spirit of the movement and the Chicano culture. The movement was also cross-generational; that is, people of various ages participated. Because so many participated in the movement, it is difficult to present an exhaustive list of these women. This matter needs to be researched in order to document female participation and preserve the accuracy of history. Some early movement women included Helen Chavez, Dolores Huerta, Ines Talamantez, and Lea Ybarra in California; Jerri Gonzales, Nita Gonzales, Marcella Trujillo Lucero, and Irene Blea in Colorado; and Luz Gutierrez; Ines Hernández Tovar, and Martha Cotera in Texas.

DEMOGRAPHIC DEFINITION

Most Americans easily distinguish most Chicanas from non-Chicanas, for there is much color and physical diversity among these women as well as much cultural diversity. Some are arid desert people, whereas others are mountain or coastal people. While most Latinas live on the mainland, others such as the Cubans and Puerto Ricans originate from islands. A physical definition goes beyond the stereotypical long dark hair, large brown eyes, and smooth tan skin to a physical location on maps. Chicanas are concentrated in the southwestern part of the country and on the Pacific Coast in southern California. Other southwestern

Table 3.1
U.S. Latino Population by State

California	34.4	New Jersey	3.3
Texas	19.4	Arizona	3.1
New York	9.0	New Mexico	2.6
Florida	7.0	Colorado	1.9
Illinois	4.0	Massachusetts	1.3

Source: U.S. Department of Commerce, Bureau of the Census. *We the American Hispanics.* November, 1933, pp. 2–3.

states include Texas, Arizona, New Mexico, and Colorado, part of the vast territory acquired by the United States as a result of the war with Mexico. But pockets of Chicanos can also be found in Chicago, Minneapolis-St. Paul, and the Akimbo Valley in Washington State. Latinos live in every state of the union. Many Cubans thrive in Miami, Florida, and many Puerto Ricans live in New York, New Jersey, and other Atlantic coast states (see Tables 3.1 and 3.2).

The exact number of Chicanas and Latinas living in the United States is not known because they are identified differently by different counting agencies. The United States Census (1993) estimates that there are roughly 22 million Latinos. Of these, more than 50 percent are female. The exact number fluctuates because of the migrant population and because of the large undocumented immigrant rate. These women are frequently referred to as wetbacks, or *mojadas*, because they had to get wet when sneaking across the U.S.-Mexican border into the United States without immigration papers. But there is no truth to this designation. Latinas frequently fly, drive, or are driven across the border. Coming across borders without official documents constitutes illegal entry, but many do enter legally on student and tourist visas.

Those women who cross the border endure severe social, psychological, and spiritual consequences. They come not only from Mexico but also from Costa Rica, Nicaragua, Guatemala, El Salvador, Chile, Argentina, Peru, Ecuador, and Colombia. Once across the border, they are labeled, confined, and coerced into remaining in "their place" as immigrants forever, afraid to seek U.S. citizenship (Table 3.3).

These women are also defined with indigenous members of their country of origin in Central and South America. For example, it is said that in 1502 Christopher Columbus "discovered" Nicaragua. The truth is that the Americas did not need discovering. They were already discovered and inhabited by ancient civilizations like the Incas and the Mayan. The difference is that Spanish colonialism was established and lasted into this very century.

Nicaragua, which contributed 15.3 percent of Central America's im-

Table 3.2
U.S. Latino Population by U.S. Metro Areas

Los Angeles–Long Beach, California	1,733,796
Riverside–San Bernardino, California	563,011
Miami–Hialeah, Florida	521,449
Anaheim–Santa Ana, California	289,690
San Diego, California	255,882
Houston, Texas	242,269
Oakland, California	207,200
McAllen–Edinburg–Mission, Texas	184,576
Chicago, Illinois	174,996
Washington, D.C.–Maryland–W. Virginia	168,140

Source: U.S. Department of Commerce, *American Demographics.* Washington, D.C., April 1993.

migration to the United States in 1993, sought to overthrow successive dictatorships in 1979. A revolution led by the Sandinista National Liberation Front (FSLN) ousted Anastasio Somoza, whose family controlled as much as 40 percent of the country's economy. Women's participation in that revolution seems to far surpass that of men. According to Maxine Fisher (1989), women fought in the front lines and were also undercover agents, participated in establishing a new government after the overthrow of the old regime, organized agricultural workers, and created more government-sponsored day care.

Fisher also estimates that 75 percent of the assembly lines in Mexico, the Caribbean, and all of Latin America were populated by women, who produced everything from clothing to packaged strawberries, baseballs, and sophisticated electronic equipment. Nicaragua has had its share of labor struggles. Women there are concentrated in the lowest paid work picking strawberries, with no contract, no benefits, no social security, and no union at a monthly salary of $51 (66 cents an hour, or 25 cents per crate) (Fisher, 1989). U.S. Chicanas and Latinas have intimate knowledge of this life, for they or their mothers have done similar work for similar pay in the United States. They have lived with wages that vary drastically from month to month, in unsafe, unclean environments, with no benefits.

Unlike Nicaragua, Argentina, which has contributed 9.7 million immigrants from South America, is a highly urban, industrialized, and literate country. Paraguay, on the other hand, is rural, has a low literacy rate, and high fertility rates. In the mid-1980s, women from Paraguay worked on the land and in agricultural jobs, but they also earned wages.

Women often trade labor-intensive rural work for exploitation in factories. Educational and economic gaps between males and females are international, but the higher the education the more women will work for wages outside the home in most countries. In Chile, the gender gap

Table 3.3
Latinas by Country of Origin

CENTRAL AMERICA

Mexico	61.2
Salvador	42.7
Guatemala	20.3
Nicaragua	15.3
Honduras	9.9
Panama	7.0
Costa Rica	4.3

SOUTH AMERICA

Colombia	36.6
Ecuador	18.5
Peru	16.9
Argentina	9.7
Chile	6.6

ISLANDS

Puerto Rico	12.1
Cuba	4.8
Dominican Republic	2.4

Source: U.S. Department of Commerce, Economics and Statistics Administration, Bureau of the Census, *We the American Hispanics.* Washington, D.C., 1993, p. 4.

is evident. Women who drop out of secondary school have the same chance of getting a semiskilled job as does a man who did not complete primary school.

In the United States, educational attainment varies among different Latino groups. Those who identified themselves as Spaniards to the U.S. Census (1993) had the highest rate of graduation from high school (77 percent). About 44 percent of Mexicans, 53 percent of Puerto Ricans, and 57 percent of Cubans had a high school diploma or higher. Roughly 46 percent of Central Americans and 71 percent of South Americans received a high school diploma or higher in 1990.

Not all Latinas live on the mainland. As mentioned earlier, Puerto Rican women are island women and have long been involved in their country's struggle for independence, especially between 1950 and 1960. Large numbers of women who immigrate from the island countries work as domestics and as private child-care providers in the homes of more affluent U.S. women. Some of these domestic workers have high school or professional degrees in their country of origin, but they leave these careers seeking other opportunities. The stereotype of Chicanas and Latinas is that they are lazy, unintelligent, and sexually irresponsible, which leads to a high teenage pregnancy rate and high welfare dependence.

These labels place U.S. Latinas at the lowest level of the country's social hierarchy, with very little social space for upward mobility.

My preliminary research among immigrant women reveals that they do not move around their U.S communities from their homes as much as do men. There is a need for research as to why. Furthermore, an analysis of labels such as immigrant, nonimmigrant, Latina, and Chicana shows that the labels have fragmented some elements of the Chicana/Latina feminist agenda.

Most Chicanas are poor or working class. Characteristically, they live isolated or far away from the Anglo communities near freeways, railroad tracks, industrial corridors, airports, or dump sites. The majority live in barrios, which implies an existence dominated by poverty, drugs, gangs, bad odors, crowded housing, and small deteriorated business sections distant from the larger central city. But not all Chicanas and Latinas should be relegated to this class. A number of them can be more broadly defined as bicultural and bilingual. They encompass vendors and businesswomen, cleaning women, clerical workers, and college students. Not only are two languages spoken, but they frequently write in either Spanish or English, or both. They are traditional but also highly creative, and nontraditional. These women are in charge of food purchasing (although men also purchase food), as well as food preparation and storage. They like music, dancing, and laughter. They value marriage, celebrate births, baptism, first holy communion, and confirmation, and mourn divorce, drugs, alcohol abuse, domestic and gang violence, and death.

Immigrant women are more isolated than Chicanas. Sometimes Chicanos and Chicanas add to the segregation of immigrant females because they have internalized hierarchical thinking and see the immigrant as lower than themselves. Perhaps this soothes the consciousness of some low-ranking Chicanas. Not all Chicanos think and act in this way. In fact, they frequently intermarry with immigrant men. Many have immediate relatives, such as grandparents, who are immigrants. In matters of racism, they endure in common; a strong emotional attachment is therefore sometimes evident.

Many Chicanas love their neighborhoods of origin; they rarely stop identifying with them because chances are that they grew up in them. Those who originate in east, west, or south-central Los Angeles talk at length about their youth and how the city has changed. Those born and raised in Barellas, in Albuquerque, New Mexico, lament the loss of their neighborhood. Those who grew up in Bessemer in Pueblo, Colorado, the north side or Five Points in Denver, or the west side of San Antonio, Texas, identify strongly with their neighborhoods long after they have left them for middle-class homes. The neighborhoods, *los vecinos*, have contributed greatly to their self-definition, and they go ''home'' as often as possible.

The social and physical space of la Chicana and la Latina, goes beyond the boundaries characteristically presented by the media. If one believed what television alone portrays, one would think that Chicano communities are riddled with negativity. They are not. Chicana feminists constantly guard against the propagation of such images. Most but not all Latinos, including Chicanos, live together in barrios; but they can also be found in middle-class communities and even in the upper-class communities of the nation. Women who make up these communities come from diverse backgrounds, originating in any of the Latino countries, and they may be of mixed heritage. Even though most Latinos in the United States are urban, not all Latinas are. Many are scattered throughout the rural areas of this nation.

Implied in a definition of Chicanas and Latinas is a political connotation driven by the fact that historically persons in the Chicano community have been confined to geographical and social space, but they have also been defined by psychological and emotional conditions by both external and internal forces. This space also has spiritual dimensions, as discussed below; for now a discussion of the impact of social isolation and discrimination on this largest ethnic group is in order.

POLITICAL IMPACT

According to popular estimates, between 15 and 21 million Latinos live in the United States. Their median age is only 26.7 years. By the year 2015, Latinos will outnumber African Americans by 44.0 million to 43.1 million, (U.S. Census, 1993). This number is ambiguous because of the unknown migrant population, and because a large number of individuals from other countries are in the United States without immigration papers and need to hide from government authorities. In 1990, Latinos were the fastest growing segment of the nation's population (U.S. Bureau of Census, 1993), constituting almost 9 percent of the nation's nearly 250 million people. Between 1980 and 1990 the Latino population grew over seven times as rapidly as the rest of the nation. The Mexicans account for the largest percentage of the Latino population, nearly doubling in size between 1970 and 1980, and then nearly doubling again in 1990. In 1990, nearly nine of every ten Latinos lived in ten states, but they were concentrated in California, Texas, New York, and Florida. Large numbers of Chicanos are scattered in the Midwest, mostly in Illinois.

With the exception of Chicana, most labels of identity have been imposed by outside entities of power, such as the U.S. government. More germane to the discussion of identity are historical factors. Until 1821 Chicana ancestors who were not Indian were called Spanish. In 1821, Mexico liberated itself from Spain. After liberation from Spain, they were called Mexicans, and later they sought control of French Mexico. Herein are rooted two periods of major significance to Chicanas of Mexican origin: the 16th of September and the Cinco de Mayo. In 1848, Mexicans became Americans, and in the 1960s they adopted the self-proclaimed label, Chicano. But in various regions of the United States they have continued to be called Spanish surnamed, Mexican Americans, Hispanics, and, more recently, Latinos.

The group is a racial group, half Indian, half European Caucasian, and is made up of ethnic people practicing a distinct culture. They have been members of a conquering race dominated by males, and they have been the conquered, dominated Indian women who worked in their conqueror's kitchens, fields, and churches. They are products of violence and rape; thus, they are a product of contradiction. Nevertheless, these women have survived to sort through all the labels, hierarchical categories, contradictory history, and oppression. Having been squeezed through a psychic sieve, they have gathered the strands at the other end to emerge strong. No mechanism in the dominant society enables them to derive adequate self-identity. They must look to their own culture to draw physical, psychological, and spiritual strength and somehow emerge whole, redefining themselves in response to historical circumstance.

Because of these historical conditions, Chicanas sometimes have life decisions to make that are different from other U.S. women. They balance the combined factors of racism and sexism in their lives and decide how "Mexican" or "Latina" they will allow their children to be. Some wonder what will happen to them if they do not marry, or have sex with a woman. Does this destroy Chicano culture? What is their cultural responsibility?

From this mental and spiritual burden the Chicano woman creates Chicana feminist consciousness poetry, plays, and university classes based on her experience. She does not define herself in economic terms. She has learned from those who came before her. She nourishes her center, and stabilizes herself as powerful just the way she is. She is spiritually whole like la curandera (healer). Her power is like that of la bruja (sorceress of the night) and should be feared. She is loving like the sacred virgin. She must teach this to as many women and men as possible, so that life for them will be different.

The Chicano civil rights movement in the 1960s put some closure to the search for identity by integrating Mexican and American history. It reconstituted spirituality and social reality into something Chicanas could relate to. The 1960s integrated being of Mexican origin, Spanish speaking, and American into something positive. Because not everyone was involved in the Chicano movement and because not everyone has a full understanding of it, not all women recognize themselves as Chicana or as members of the homeland, Aztlan. In fact, some women define themselves as descendants of the Spanish conquistadors who colonized the Indians of Mexico, and they want no association with low-ranking Indians. These women prefer the term *Spanish* or *Hispanic* when they self-identify.

The Mexican immigrant female, the largest proportion of the group, prefers the term *Mexicana* or *Mexican American*, depending on when she immigrated into the country; others prefer Latina. Government officials use the term *Hispanic* to refer to the Latino population. None of the terms, however, differentiates the differences in race and ethnicity among the diverse population.

Approximately 61 percent of the Latino population prefer the term *Chicano* when they are self-identifying. This population is highly concentrated in the Southwest, but can also be found in other parts of the nation (U.S. Bureau of Census, 1993). Some southwestern Mexican Americans are, indeed, descendants of the earliest European settlers in the United States. They were absorbed into the United States as the result of the U.S. war with Mexico and the signing of the Treaty of Guadalupe Hidalgo in 1848. Among them are those who came to the United States to escape the Mexican Revolution in 1910. The next immigrant group is predominantly male and immigrated via the Bracero Program (1942 to 1947). These men came alone as "guest workers" and later brought women and children to the country. The most recent immigrant group is a result of the push–pull economic and political relationship between U.S. Central and Latin America. Many Latinas enter the United States from Guatemala, Ecuador, Chile, and Peru. These immigrant females inherited the conquered status of Chicanas as the result of the Mexican War, and they are treated as conquered people by the dominant society.

GEOGRAPHICAL DIFFERENCES

Chicana female ancestors suffered isolation in the Southwest. Great physical distance separated them from the central valley of Mexico, where modern life was lived; there was also a vast social gulf between Mexicanas and white women. In the early 1800s, the large region consisted of the male-dominated mission system and the military. Some Mexicanas lived on church property, government land holdings, or *estancias* (very large properties), *haciendas* (private estates), and *ranchos* (ranches).

Contemporary Chicanas are the product of different settlement patterns and geographical conditions. Some have long histories of urban living. Others are rural, living in deserts or mountains. Still others are coastal persons. Indian and colonial women who settled in the state of California, for example, experienced conditions specific to mission life and the coastal region. In 1542, Spanish seamen, without women, first landed on the coast with ships loaded with cargo from India and China.

They were sailing to Mexico. Later expeditions were sent into the region by the viceroy of Nueva España. The earliest settlers encountered bays along the coast, which were given both male and female Catholic saint names such as San Diego and Santa Barbara. Settlers with women did not return until a century and half later, when Spain was informed that Russian ships were landing on the northern coast hunting for otters and seals. This settlement expedition brought Catholic clergy and the mission system. The Spanish Crown founded a total of twenty-one missions along the entire coast of California.

In Arizona, a less intense mission structure existed. Southern Colorado is much like New Mexico, but New Mexico had a larger indigenous population. New Mexico now has nineteen recognized Indians tribes, among whom the Navaho and Zuni are the largest. A review of Spanish and Indian settlement patterns should not overlook the fact that the Spanish had early strongholds in what is now Florida and that they controlled the Mississippi River trade, but indigenous people lived there first. Prior to the coming of the Spanish, indigenous people had already explored and settled many regions. They had contact with other tribes and were knowledgeable about the land, the weather, the fauna, and ways to survive. In some regions, the Spanish/Indian conflict was less intense, and cultural exchange took place. When the Anglo came, conflict characterized most, if not all, the previous settlements because the Anglo brought a different language, a different way of relating to land and the animals, a different way of living, and a different religion. Anglos ultimately established their own settlement patterns, but many settled in Spanish-speaking communities.

During this time, female and male labor was strictly divided. Some of the large Spanish, and later Mexican, land grants were given by the Spanish crown directly to women like Doña María del Carmen Calvillo, who managed ranches they had inherited from their husbands or fathers (National Women's History Project, 1992). How women both individually and in groups coped with the racial conflict is not well documented, although it is known that arranged marriages were a norm in both cultures and that intermarriage was a vehicle through which rich Mexican men dealt with the economic imposition of Anglo men. For example, only Mexican citizens could buy land. Anglo males could become citizens by marrying Mexican women. Mexican fathers frequently arranged the intermarriages in order to increase, or at least to sustain, their land grant holdings.

In what we now call Texas, conflict arose over the Anglo refusal to live according to Mexican law and the specific conditions under which Texans were allowed to live in Mexico's northern territory. War followed. Much attention has been given to the battle of the Alamo, a small mission in a row of missions near San Antonio, founded by María Betancour. The Texans lost this battle but won a later battle, making them an independent entity that quickly joined the Anglo-dominated United States.

Life for colonial women centered around the home and church. In the small villages adjacent to the missions, women's work, especially that of *enjaradoras*, was essential. *Enjaradoras* were women who plastered and replastered the exteriors of adobe houses, churches, and other public buildings by hand in order to protect them from severe weather conditions.

At the mission of San Gabriel near Los Angeles, no one's work was more essential than that of Eulalia Perez. Her descendants still live nearby, and they are proud of the fact that Perez lived at the Mission de San Gabriel with her children between 1821 and 1835 and was the keeper of the mission keys. Perez managed all the mission supplies, supervised the grinding of corn, the threshing of wheat, and the making of cheese, soap, butter, cloth, wine, and olive oil. Perez also delivered provisions to the troops and taught Indian women to card, spin wool, weave, and sew cloth in the Spanish tradition.

During the Spanish colonial period, Spanish married women apparently enjoyed many more legal rights than Anglo women living in the United States (National Women's History Project, 1992; Veyna, 1986). They retained control of property, held half-interest in all property shared with husbands, and could purchase and sell crops and animals. They could operate businesses, enter into contracts in their own names, and bring suit to testify in court. They enjoyed personal freedoms as well. Dancing, drinking, smoking, and gambling were considered acceptable female behaviors.

While Anglo women and colonial Spanish women endured heavy dress in hot summers, the indigenous and mestiza women wore comfortable, loose-fitting clothing made of cotton. But the mestiza's freedoms were seen as weaknesses; she was labeled "loose" by both Anglo males and females.

The economic power of colonial Mexican women can be measured by reviewing the will and testament documentation of women living in New Mexico from 1744 to 1767. Angelina Veyna (1986) surveys the lists of women's material possessions, showing their purchases and disposal of possessions and property. Women owned, purchased, and disposed of quite valuable property, especially in the Rio Arriba region. They owned farm and ranch and carpenter tools, houses, stables, fields, and orchards in various locations. They also owned furniture, such as chests, stools, tables, benches, and chairs. They had a variety of clothing: mainly skirts, capes, mantillas, handkerchiefs, stockings, slips, and blankets. The clothing was made of silk, cotton, and piquin. Among decorative items were listed ribbon, lace, and fringe. Some of the women owned musical instruments like guitars and violins as well as jewelry. One woman boasted seven strands of dark pearls; another owned a coral and silver choker, some blue enamel bracelets, and some exquisite pearl earrings. Some of the women also had guns, knives, candles, and food. They owned, sold, and otherwise controlled land, and were instrumental in the transfer of land via marriage.

The women's last wills and testaments provide some insight into their relationships with the saints and the Christian pantheon of the time. Among their religious articles were prayer books, crucifixes, pictures of saints, retablos and cuadros (religious pictures of saints' carefully produced on wood), and religious statues (*bultos*). Some of the saints' images included Santa Isabel, Nuestra Señora de Dolores, Nuestra Señora del Pilar, and Nuestra Señora de los Remedios. Livestock seems to have been distributed evenly between female and male heirs. In disposing of property, even when male consent had to be secured in these transactions, it appears that it was frequently the woman who made the decision about how to dispose of her property. Not uncommonly, each spouse in a marriage claimed and disposed of his or her own property. This was done to ensure that materials were not bequeathed to inappropriate heirs. None of the documents, notes Veyna, gave the illusion that women hesitated as to how their goods were to be distributed.

Apparently, until 1848, colonial women were involved in official complaints as both complainants and defendants. They are recorded as owning property as both individuals or collectively with their spouses. According to court records, they engaged in the distribution of tools, criminal proceedings, power of attorney, estate proceedings, family disputes, land litigation, and personal complaints. Marriages, then and now, were legal contracts, and marital difficulties were frequently a topic of notarial documents. Most intermarriages took place between white men and Spanish women. Kit Carson and George Bent, for example, married the Jaramillo sisters of Taos.

The subject of personal honor was also frequently a topic to be settled in the courts. Before the Americanos entered the Southwest, Spanish women served as court witnesses as early as the second decade of the eighteenth century. Indian women were not highly visible; they were listed as servants, or criadas. (The term *criadas* has a far different meaning today in the contemporary New Mexican context; criadas are female children who are not natural children, and are reared as if they were natural children. This takes place without formal adoption papers.)

The court testimony of early Spanish women appears to have been respected as well as that of men. Colonial men may have been more tolerant of female participation, especially of women who had real power. Perhaps, too, women were more assertive then. Veyna's research (1986) reports only one complaint about the negative treatment of women in the courts. The lack of complaints may be due to the fact that women did not dare complain—or could it be that there was less to complain about? The record is not clear, but does offer some support for maintaining that women had more resources and more respect prior to the arrival of the Americanos.

During this period, many women died in childbirth, but there was a large widow population in the urban areas. Remarriage by widows was rare, but when they did remarry, they often married older men who sometimes died and left them widowed once again. Widowhood often led to an accumulation of property in the rural areas. Life was more difficult on the frontier, and rarely did women outlive men. It was not unusual for a male to bury two, even three, wives.

A great majority of the population was illiterate, especially the women, but some women were able to write, and they signed their names on various documents.

Since the Spaniards were the ruling elite, they recorded their own history at the exclusion of the indigenous, who are mentioned in marriage records and in *deligencias*—required testimonials stating that the couple was free from other obligations and able to marry. The deligencia required witnesses to declare that the intended were not promised in marriage or married to anyone else. The social prescriptions for marriage are witnessed in the well-established New Mexican tradition of the *Entriega de Novios*. This secular custom took place during a marriage reception. The bride and groom were presented to the society as a married couple, and in front of this society they were instructed on how to behave in marriage. The ritual was a musical composition at the time of presentation, a very unique practice that gave highly egalitarian practical and spiritual advice.

Ever since the Anglo invasion of Mexico and the signing of the Treaty of Guadalupe Hidalgo in 1848, Chicanos and Indians have resisted Anglo influence. It was not until after World War II that Chicano male consciousness solidified in some southwestern regions and Chicanos began concentrated efforts to change their quality of life in order to define themselves and secure a future. Many women were involved in the League of United Latin American Citizens (LULAC), which was formed after World War II. This organization struggles against racism and women have always participated. The name of Alicia Montemayor, an outspoken feminist, is closely associated with this advocacy organization.

Chicano and Chicana consciousness was at a high in the 1960s, when the Chicano civil rights movement put labels like prejudice, racism, sexism, and discrimination on how they had been treated in the United States. Naming the process motivated action and cries of revolution that crystallized in a reform movement. This struggle and those of the women who came before them motivated Chicanas to address women's issues in the Chicano civil rights movement.

PSYCHOLOGICAL DEFINITION

To various degrees, the Chicana's life has been characterized by struggle, a learned response rooted in a history of resistance and revolution. It is a social-historical fact that Chicano ancestors in Mexico revolted against Spain and France, defended themselves against the United States, endured the Mexican Revolution (more thoroughly discussed in Chapter 5), and that their descendants continue to resist American imposition. This resistance to social, cultural, political, and spiritual domination is a struggle for space, a place in society that is not always at the lowest rung of the social ladder. It is a struggle for better living conditions and better social treatment; it is also a struggle for healthy psychological and spiritual space not only for Chicanos but also for their oppressors. Herein, the Chicana struggled to be better defined, accepted, and respected without having to negotiate away her culture. She did this not only for herself as a woman, but also for her community, her people. La Chicana has a genuine sense of "her people." It is in her community that she has been conditioned, learning to love and to appreciate the meaning of family, neighbors, and the environment. Her community is a creative place, with boundaries, some good and some negative. In her community she was socialized with strong segregation messages that created a mentality that did not allow women to go beyond the community's borders into other parts of the city, other schools, or other restaurants and prohibited them from seeking a career or alternative sexual orientation. In this physical space, women constantly face homophobia, racism, sexism, and class discrimination. Some Latino communities are places where women can enjoy reasonable, comfortable lives; most are not as comfortable. Women balance poverty with their fears of drive-by shootings, break-ins, muggings, and rape, usually at the hands of their own men. In some communities, they do not have to leave the boundaries to interact with Anglos. They do not even need to know how to speak English. Other communities are more interdependent and more interactive. Women leave them everyday to work, to go to the doctor, community college or university, and to visit relatives.

The objective of Chicana feminism is to expand the severely limited space available to the Chicana. Whereas Latinas demand that the United States take note of discrimination against them and their community, Chicana feminists focus on the particular prejudice against women of their community. This prejudice both from outside of and within their community disempowers women both in the dominant society and in their own culture.

What little the Chicana knows about her history has affected her attitude and behavior in her own country, and she is now ready to share that attitude with the rest of the world. Her limited presence at the U.N. international women's conferences in China attests to this readiness. In China, and all over the United States, Chicanas and other Latinas are speaking out about what minority social status in the United States means, even though they are not the numerical minority. They are stating the significance of their cultural group as part of that nation's 200 million population. For thirty years they have been reporting how the dominant culture maligns them within their own culture. They frequently present themselves as victims, and they are learning how to stress their unique survival skills and their contributions to the world, and they continue to demand more flexibility in a rigid society. In this effort, they have struggled to give voice to their own definition of themselves, and they have succeeded.

Any definition of la Chicana requires that we recognize that Chicanas are indigenous to the hemisphere. When scholars, the media, and the general public talk about Latinas, they give little attention to the indigenous past and to gender differentials. These omissions have added to the historical trauma of the Chicana psyche in a way that is frequently undetected. They negate the Chicana, making her invisible and unimportant. They silence her. The response to this violation is personal spiritual retreat and trust in the spiritual balance of the world. *No hay mal que bien no venga* is an old saying that means that something bad cannot happen without something good happening as a result of it.

Chicanas are mestizas, women of mixed blood, who have not been taught their history and way of life. Because of their Spanish ancestors and the atrocities the Spanish committed against the Indians, many Indian people do not want to recognize Chicanos as indigenous. Most Chicanas have been identified, through patriarchal tradition, with the Spanish European male and have taken Spanish surnames and have absorbed the Spanish tradition. In addition, the dominant Anglo culture is pressuring the Chicana to assimilate and to give up her culture and be like other dominant cultural members. Either she cannot do this because it offends her spirit, or she will not do it for political reasons, or for both. However, much of the culture is indigenous and is blended. Chicanas have been taught not to value indigenousness, not to recognize the indigenousness of their culture by both external and internal forces. Nevertheless, some of the strongest influences are indigenous, and they especially appear in the spirituality of the women.

SPIRITUAL DEFINITION

The strongest spiritual figures in Chicano culture are female: La Virgen de Guadalupe (the Indian-Spanish Catholic mother of Jesus Christ and the patron saint of Mexico), la llorona (the wailing woman with historical roots in the Spanish conquest of Mexico), la bruja (the powerful sorceress or witch, who like la llorona has both Indian and Spanish origins), and la curandera (the influential healer who uses Indian medicine and Catholicism). These forceful women are part of the spiritual and material world, controlling life, death, destruction, healing, and restitution by manipulating forces that are both from the spiritual and the material.

Power is an important concern for Chicana feminists because they live in a powerful material reality; their country engages in vigorous oppression and so potent responses are required. Their country also promises the best in the world. The truth of the matter is that most Chicanas and Latinas have unrealized power that they have been raised to believe does not exist. They have been taught to recognize only power that is male or white both in the material world and in the emotional and spiritual realm. This sense of power is suppressed in females, and they are made materially powerless by the individualistic, upwardly mobile, profit-oriented, competitive world around them.

Chicanas know that a life centered on competition, individualism, aspiration for upward mobility, and profit is spiritually devoid for them. A certain brand of spirituality is necessary for Chicanas. Without a sense of spirituality that is balanced with the social and historical realities of their people, they might feel psychologically unbalanced and desire more material things. When these things are acquired, they may still be unfulfilled. This line of thinking is in keeping with the work of Thomas Moore's *Care of the Soul* (1992), but whereas most Anglos think they have only this one life to live, Chicanas generally believe in an afterlife. They do not feel they have to get as much as they can while they can.

Chicanas are heavily influenced by the dominant way of thinking, but well-adjusted women do not live their individual daily lives manipulated by competition and a search for upward mobility. They are linked to a world that is much larger than they. They resist being controlled by a life of purchasing material things. They know that the society functions by getting people to buy products and services, and they know that this exchange mode has been transformed into a model of social interaction. This model undermines the spiritual dimension of humans, which is not good. It upsets the balance between humans and nature because in order to continue producing goods for profit nature is violated. Chicanas, like their indigenous sisters, believe they are on earth to tend the resources; the resources do not tend them, and resources do not exist for men to use up and abuse.

Chicanas have seen how Anglos make laws that appear to be contrary to the Chicana's cultural life. Both Christianity and the government have taught them that people are equal, and they believe it. But they know, personally, that white men have formulated laws and policies making some humans more equal than others. Chicanas have seen Chicano men trying to emulate white men. They are keenly aware of the hypocrites among the men who control their homes, Christian churches, and governments. They have witnessed how the predominantly Christian U.S. culture does not esteem Latinos, the immigrant, the street person, the drug addict. Chicanas know that the dominant culture will not protect Latino communities from gang violence by dealing with the problems that cause gang violence. They see how drugs in their communities are dealt with as if they were a criminal problem, and not a social or health issue. They also see how gays and lesbians are treated negatively, especially if they are people of color. Chicanas also know that white people, especially those in control, "talk a good line" but do not act on what they say. They note when white men do not fund social programs that will eliminate discrimination and prejudice, and they have observed how men in control do not acknowledge the connection among all aspects of life: the historical, social, political, psychological, and spiritual. Chicanas know that U.S. society is hierarchical and compartmentalized; how the dominant culture practices situational ethics, and how it ensures the white male's right to pick and choose how they act by supporting the separations of spirituality, psychology, and the material from the political and from the cultural. Chicanas know that a true Christian does not tolerate an injustice; yet, injustices take place every moment of every day and night. Even the Catholic Church, which has been supported by Latinos for centuries, does not step in to end injustice against Latinos.

White men in control of education do not attempt to control the flow of information and to ensure that women's knowledge is recorded, taught, and utilized. White men have not stopped the manipulation and control of the media and the top to bottom government decisions that affect women, but one cannot expect the oppressor to liberate. Chicanas know they have to liberate themselves. They are frustrated and angered by the need to impose moral and social order. Dominant men have ruined the social order by allowing racism and sexism to fester. Chicanas ponder whether they should even try to help white men and some white women to find a new reason for being. As Thomas Moore has shown, they know that one cannot find meaning by dichotomizing, categorizing, and creating hierarchies and conflict.

Chicana spirituality has to do with being connected to reality at the material and spiritual levels. It cannot be totally measured because so much of it is subjective. It is a personal language and a personal realization that an enormous entity communicates with the individual, and that the individual communicates with it. It is powerful, and it is related to the individual, uniting us. Like la Virgen de Guadalupe, the indigenous deity, it loves us and provides all we need. Like the pain of la llorona, the weeping woman searching for children, it hurts when others tear at what is sacred to Chicanas. The Chicana's spirituality is the glory of the vastness of the sky and its ability to change color in its relationship to the sun. It is the greenness of the wondrous plants and how they live and die. It is the fiery force of the radiant sun, the luminous light of the moon, the preciousness of crystalline air, the brilliance of flowers and words, the immensity of the power of the land, living beings. It is not man at the top of the evolutionary scale.

REFERENCES

Anaya, Rudolfo A. 1986. *Chicano in China*. Albuquerque: University of New Mexico Press.

Associated Press. 1990. *China: From the Long March to Tiananmen Square*. New York: Henry Holt and Co.

Baca-Zinn, Maxine. 1975a. "Chicanas: Power and Control in the Domestic Sphere." *De colores* 1, no. 3: pp. 19–31.

———. 1975b. "Political Familism: Toward Sex Role Equality in Chicano Families." *Aztlan: Chicano Journal of the Social Sciences and the Arts* 6 (Spring): pp. 13–26.

Blea, Irene I. 1995. *Researching Chicano Communities: Social-Historical, Physical, Psychological, and Spiritual Space*. New York: Praeger.

Castillo, Ana. 1995. *Massacre of the Dreamers: Essays on Xicanisma*. Albuquerque: University of New Mexico Press.

Cheng, Nien. 1987. *Life and Death in Shanghai*. New York: Grove Press; New York: Books on Tape, 1987.

Encuentro Femenil. 1974. *Encuentro Femenil: The First Chicana Feminist Journal*. Los Angeles: Hijas de Cuauhtemoc.

Fisher, Maxine P. 1989. *Women in the Third World*. New York: Franklin Watts.

Hotz, Robert Lee. 1995. "Is Concept of Race a Relic?" *Los Angeles Times*, April 15, 1995, pp. 1, 14.

Moore, Thomas. 1992. *Care of the Soul*. New York: HarperCollins; Recorded Books, 1994.

National Women's History Project. 1992. "Adelante Mujeres." (Video.) Washington, D.C.

Tuchman, Barbara Wertheim. 1986. *Notes from China*. Charlotte Hall, Md.: Recorded Books, 1986.

Veyna, Angelina F. 1986. "Women in Early New Mexico: A Preliminary View." In T. Cordova et al., eds., *Chicana Voices: Intersections of Class, Race and Gender*. Austin: CMAS Publications, University of Texas Press.

Ybarra, Leonarda. 1977. "Conjugal Role Relationships in the Chicano Family." Ph.D. diss., University of California, Berkeley.

———. 1982, February. "When Wives Work: The Impact on the Chicano Family." *Journal of Marriage and the Family*, No. 44, pp. 169–178.

4

CULTURAL SOVEREIGNTY

The Fourth World Women's Conference demonstrated that cultural sovereignty is an issue for many women around the world. Cultural sovereignty is like tribal sovereignty. Most indigenous people of the Americas want the right to govern themselves. Implied in this desire is the goal of practicing their culture undisturbed by the eurocentric governments that so frequently dominate them. Among Chicanas, in the 1960s, there was much talk about Chicanos governing themselves, but this does not appear to be the case in the late 1990s. But Chicanas do want recognition of their people, more freedom to practice their culture, and much less discrimination within the context of the existing government. On their own land they want to be free to wear certain hairstyles, articles of clothing, jewelry, and cosmetics without being ridiculed, stared at, or commented upon as not being dressed for success.

At the United Nations' women's conference, other indigenous women spoke about this matter, and about how they seek liberation from ethnic cleansing that goes beyond killing people. For them, ethnic cleansing extends into killing the culture of those who have managed to stay alive. Among those who spoke were women from Tibet, Israel, Italy, Mongolia, and Peru. In Peru the struggle to reconceptualize itself in a more indigenous manner is linked to the controversial Sendero Luminoso. (In English, this is inappropriately translated as the Shining Path; a more accurate translation is the Luminous Torch.) The Sendero Luminoso,

A high school student keeps in touch with indigenous roots by engaging in Aztec dancing. Photograph by Oscar Castillo.

guerrilla terrorism, and government intervention in the lives of the indigenous have spurred massive migration to the cities of Gamarra, Cuzco, and Lima. (The Sendero Luminoso should not be confused with the Movimiento Revolucinario Tupac Amaru (MRTA), which was responsible for the hostage situation in Lima in December 1996.)

Chicanas are sensitive to the idea of cultural sovereignty and ethnic liberation because of their colonized past and the fact that they and their people have sought freedom. The contradiction is that they are products of the conqueror and the conquered.

INDIGENOUS WOMEN

The Chicana feminist perspective on her own indigenous nature concentrates on pre-Columbian periods and stresses cultural practices that are still adhered to today. This concentration also suggests that perhaps periods of significance do not have the same meaning for men as they do for women, or that how men conceptualize the world is only one way of looking at the world. In the dominant society, for example, Chicanas inherit a hierarchically stratified culture that compartmentalizes and dichotomizes people and things into good and bad categories. In this scheme women, especially Latinas, severely lack value.

Entire civilizations had existed in the Americas prior to the appearance of the Spaniards. The earliest of them is represented by the Olmec. The Olmecas cultivated rubber and tobacco and carved in stone, and may have had a powerful, mystical society, with oracles. The Olmec originated in the middle preclassic period on the Gulf Coast and are symbolized by giant, gray, hand-carved heads. The artifacts of this period are telling. They provide information about physical type, dress, ornaments, cranial deformation, tattooing, hair styles, and body and facial painting. Inhabitants worshiped natural phenomena and fertility. Many symbols of fertility have been found and are thought to have been offerings for a good harvest. The Olmec originated in the state of Tabasco and the southern portion of the state of Veracruz, in Mexico. Theirs was a strongly stratified Mesoamerican class society.

Mesoamerica is the region north of Central America, which begins in what today is known as Yucatan, Mexico, and in which a process of continuous cultural development has taken place. Major important urban centers have appeared in this region. It is customary to divide this cultural development into three major eras: the preclassic (1700–200 B.C.); the classic (200 B.C.–A.D. 9); and the postclassic (A.D. 900 until the landing of the Spanish). Each era is divided into shorter periods. The class stratification of the Olmec, however, should be questioned and analyzed for eurocentric cultural biases.

Olmec influence was so widespread that it has been considered the "mother culture" of the Americas. Olmecas are credited for having conceptualized the concept of zero, which was later discovered to be used widely by the Mayan. The Olmeca artistic style produced elongated skulls resulting from purposeful cranial deformation plus turned-down, feline-style mouths with lips that curl downward. Ana Castillo (1995) romanticizes the period and interprets it as a society of mystics and oracles that are part of the Chicano cultural inheritance. It was extinguished by the Spanish European, who arrived on the continent in the 1540s. In Castillo's interpretation, the ability to produce oracles and mystics was nearly extinguished when the Chicanos were conquered by the Anglos in 1848, and finally when they were assimilated into the dominant culture.

The Olmec influence on Mayan development is strongly evident. The Mayans maintained a common identity via a common language and some very basic characteristics. They occupied the territory from the Grijalva River in the state of Tabasco, Mexico, to the present-day republics of Honduras, El Salvador, Guatemala, and Belize in Central America. Many U.S. Latinas emigrate from these countries and have brought the remnants of these cultures with them. The best examples of relics from

Mesoamerica and the pre-Columbian period can be seen in the National Museum of Anthropology in Mexico City (see also Gomez-Tagle, 1985). There one can experience a Jaina figurine representing an indigenous woman with a fine cotton huipil (garment), elaborate hairstyle, and facial decoration consisting of scarification on the chin and between the eyebrows. From Yaxchilan, Chiapas, a lintel or slab depicts a ruler and another woman holding a bundle. It has been interpreted that they are carrying out an important transaction and that the women controlled resources. Another lintel from the same place and the late classic period reveals a ruler of the jaguar lineage holding a scepter. Facing him is a woman, also of high rank, attired in another beautiful huipil offering him the cord for autosacrifice.

The later preclassic period reveals more variety in form and decoration. There is reflected an influence from the northern areas indicating that people traveled. During this period, tools appear for the first time. Hammers, plumb bobs, chisels, and perforators indicate a high level of technological development. It is difficult to speculate what activities women participated in. This is due to the cultural socialization and indoctrination of the contemporary mind which has difficulty detaching itself from current values and structural understandings. Beliefs and opinions about contemporary gender roles may cloud the perspective, but a stroll through the National Museum of Anthropology reveals figurines depicting stout, husky people. One such male clay figurine holds a ball of dough between his hands. This figure is from the middle preclassic period and probably depicts a propitiatory offering for good crops. Thus, male gender roles might not have been as stringent as they are for Chicanas and Latinas today.

Moving forward in time, during the Mexica (Aztec) era, one encounters Xochipilli, the "prince of the flowers," the god of song, poetry, theater, love, dance, vegetation, and spring. He sits on a throne decorated with flowers and butterflies, and wears jade ear plugs, a collar, and sandals of jaguar skin.

A study of the middle preclassic period reveals the physical characteristics of people as well as their dress, ornaments, and hairstyles. Plaits and locks of hair were common, and they could have been used either for beautification or for distinguishing the user. The period of greatest splendor, roughly the seventh century, is the Teotihuacan Period. The city of Teotihuacan had approximately 80,000 inhabitants and covered a large area of land. Its planning was outstanding with streets laid along north-south and east-west axes and houses built on cement foundations. Scholars maintain that this planning indicates the existence of a complex social, economic, and governmental system. Adorned tripod bowls with lids are typical vessels of the period. Many vessels for domestic use have been identified: enormous jars for storage, pots for cooking, amphoras with three handles used to carry water, and large braziers for burning copal incense.

During this period, there existed large painted buildings with religious motifs. Sculpture incorporated hard and semiprecious stones such as serpentine, alabaster, and quartz. A funerary mask with turquoise, serpentine, and shell incrustation gives no indication of who made it or who wore it, but without doubt it is impressive. During this late period, one encounters Coyolxauhqui, goddess of the moon, who was sister of Huitzilopochitli, the god of war. Coyolxauhqui is known as "she of the face painted with rattles." The snakes gave rise to her Nahuatl name. (Nahuatl was the language of the Aztecs, the Mexica who came to the central valley of Mexico from Aztlan, their region of origin far to the north in the southwestern part of what is now the United States. Coyolli signifies rattles in Nahuatl.) The Mexicas occupied the city of Tenochtitlan in 1325. By the time the Spaniards arrived two centuries later, they controlled a very powerful empire. They are said to have been a warlike and conquering people who came from Aztlan and managed to subjugate, either directly or by commercial means, nations as distant as the Huastecs from the Gulf Coast of Mexico as well as the Zapotecs and Mixtecs of Oaxaca. The Aztecs collected tribute from the most distant and varied regions. Cocoa beans served as currency, but most transactions were made in kind. Some of these subjugated people were the first to ally themselves with the Spaniards in order to overthrow the Mexicas. From this period in Mexican history comes the fourteen-foot-high Sun Stone, or the Aztec calendar, as it is frequently referred to incorrectly. There is evidence that a female advised the calculation and building of this magnificent instrument.

Aztec women traveled with males in armies into battles serving as cooks and carriers of supplies. This practice was later duplicated in the Mexican Revolution of 1910, when often women in Azteca armies were as numerous as males (Enriquez and Mirande, 1979). At home girls received instruction in sewing and embroidery and participated in religious ceremonies. They were educated in the temples in the rituals of the priesthood and midwifery, and their studies began very early in life. They made clothing for the priests and idols and were taught by elderly priestesses. Today dressing the saints is still a woman's function. Women were represented as spiritual and mythological figures on earth and in other worlds. The universe was divided into male and female counterparts. Indeed, all things were based on male-female elements, but much can be traced to mother worship. Tonantzin, Mother Earth, was worshiped on hills and mountains. According to popular Mexican myth, the volcano Iztacihuatl is another version of Tonantzin.

Tonantzin has a viable connection to La Virgen de Guadalupe. She was worshiped on the hill of Tepeyac where La Virgen is said to have first appeared in Mexico. La Virgen is the mother of Jesus Christ, and represents a cultural merging of indigenous tradition and European elements, but cultural blending can become cultural distortion. One must question if another version of the Mexica mother, Coatlicue, mother of the gods, was not distorted over time. Not far from the Sun Stone in the Museo National de Antropologia in Mexico City, one can see the very large sculpture of Coatlicue, goddess of the earth and of life and death. She is represented as a decapitated woman from whose neck spring two serpent heads symbolizing streams of blood. She wears a necklace of hands and hearts symbolizing her insatiable thirst for human blood in the form of human sacrifice. Her hands are shown as serpent heads and her feet as eagle claws. She now appears as an antique dreadful deity, having two aspects: life giver and killer of life, fertility and death. Perhaps she most vividly depicts the dark side of the goddess, the shadow life of ourselves. It may be that all human beings have aspects that are negative. On thing is true: Coatlicue was created in the context of a war-oriented society. It is men who make war; women and children endure it.

WOMEN OF AZTLAN

During the Chicano civil rights movement of the 1960s, the Chicanos focused on the warriors of Aztlan, the Aztec, Mexica. Aztlan existed before the Spanish, before the national boundaries between Mexico and the United States were formed. The vast northern Mexican territory extends to a time when humans lived in caves, and they relied on hunting and gathering, having domesticated corn, lentils, and millet. It is the place of the indigenous origin of the last great aboriginal civilizations of Mexico. Perhaps Aztlan includes the area of Mesa Verde, among the Anasazi, and the cliff dwellings in the Four Corners of the United States, where the state lines of New Mexico, Arizona, Colorado, and Utah meet. In 1300 B.C. the Anasazi mysteriously left this site and virtually disappeared. Some scholars contend that they migrated south along the Rio Grande and settled among pueblo Indians. The heartiest wandered southward until they saw the sacred symbol of an eagle perched on a cactus, with a serpent in its mouth. Only when they saw the sacred sight did they settle. Then Indians survived to build the last of the great civilizations of Mexico in the central valley.

For Chicanas, Aztlan is the homeland. The movement symbolizes the struggle to claim a homeland and to be cultural in an Indian way. To be from Aztlan is to be political and to claim cultural sovereignty in a nation full of stereotypes about Mexicans and Chicanas. Aztlan is the battle cry, the war against the man-made boundaries that have made Aztlan a nonentity. Thus, Aztlan is a cultural and political place in which one can physically live; but it is also a spiritual place from which one can draw strength. It has a relationship to history as a physical, social, spiritual, and psychological space that has been violated. There is no room here for gender differentiation. The homeland is for all. It is feminine. It is Mother Earth. It nurtures, and it gives identity, dignity, and roots. It is a place and an idea, a behavioral way of life that fights against racism, sexism, and classism.

European explorers encountered a world that was new to them, but it was a very old world. When the Spanish came to the Americas, they discovered a world of people living with exotic fruits and vegetables, wonderful architecture, and an advanced system of medicine and healing. They encountered women and men who had created a highly sophisticated art that was incorporated into architecture and public life. The Spanish discovered astronomy, elaborate sewage systems, and mass communication among the people they inappropriately called Indians. The Spanish brought with them European motivations, ways of talking, thinking, and behaving toward women. These ways often clashed with and were destructive to native people. These ways are still with us. In our contemporary mind, the word "native" means primitive, savage, barbaric, and wild before it means "citizen." At its worst, "woman" means less than male; at its best, it means spouse of a male. Rarely does it mean "powerful," "leader," or "equal to men." Most early accounts of the Spanish explorations suggest that it was truly a man's world, that women were incidental, and that at best only one woman, Doña Marina, played a viable part in the conquest.

LA LLORONA

Instrumental to the survival of Spanish men in the Americas was the role of indigenous women. Most closely related to the history and culture of the United States is the encounter of the two in Mexico. Indigenous women had lifestyles very unlike those of the women of Spain. Their physical features were also different. They were darker in color, their attire was more casual and colorful, and their lifestyle was defined by other norms and cultural values. The importance of indigenous women to the Spanish male has been documented by contemporary Chicana scholars, who have been strongly influenced by the male-dominated curriculum of Chicano Studies. For example, language was important to indigenous women, as documented by Martha Cotera (1976) in the first nationally distributed text about Chicanas in the United States. In Aztec society, women celebrated the approaching birth of a child with poetry. They performed complicated healing and spiritual rituals that incorporated the new mother and the new child. Medical women prayed as they attended the expectant mother. The mother would speak to the unborn child in Nahuatl, praising it, and telling it of her hopes for its future.

The mother boiled herb teas similar to the ones we have today. Upon its birth the child was presented to the gods.

Some of this early Spanish and Indian history has taken on legendary and mythical forms that have remained sophisticated cultural productions. One female figure straddles the historical periods mentioned above and continues to exist today. Malintzin, Doña Marina, la malinche, and la llorona are all the same person. She appears in the paintings and writings of the best Chicano authors, and like a ghost, she emerges in plays, songs, and poetry. She appears in the Mexican-American oral tradition, as well as in written Chicana scholarship, as the oldest living female influence in the Americas. She has been seen by adult women and men, by young and old. The highly educated, the superstitious, the scientific, the religious, and the sacrilegious all attest to the existence of la llorona. She has endured the transition into high-tech society and is given major attention in my earlier writings on la Chicana (Blea, 1992). Her Nahuatl name was Malintzin, but Spaniards baptized her as Doña Marina. Even though Hernán Cortés, the man with whom she is most frequently associated, was the first to be called *malinche* or traitor, she is now referred to as la malinche: the woman who betrayed Mexico and made possible the Spanish conquest.

La malinche is frequently described as Cortés's translator and concubine. The word "concubine" implies that Doña Marina willingly participated in Cortés's adventures. But this is doubtful, for she originally came to him as a slave. It should be noted that she was barely fourteen years old. Many stories have been written about her, and much controversy exists over her role in the Spanish conquest of the Aztec Empire. The story of la llorona, its origin, and it messages have strong significance for the Spanish-speaking people of the Southwest, especially the women and children. It has taken on legendary and mythical forms with enduring and frightening symbolism that has perhaps not yet been recognized.

La llorona has had four different names from four different periods. (1) Malinalli, Malina, Malin, Malintzin, and Ixkakuk have appeared as her pre-Columbian names (Figueroa Torres, 1975); (2) Doña Marina is the name consistent with the conquest; (3) la malinche is her colonial name; and (4) she exists as la llorona to this day. The story of la llorona symbolizes three human entities—Indios, Mexicanos, and Chicanos—as well as the spirituality of Aztlan.

Malintzin was basically an intelligent, multilingual *indigena* (Indian woman), who learned to speak many languages as a young child. She had traveled throughout the Aztec Empire many times. Her father was a representative of the court of Moctezuma, and he frequently took his wife and child with him on his duties. Some scholars suspect that Malintzin might even have been Moctezuma's niece. When her father died performing the duty of the court, her mother remarried and had another child, a son. Because the first born, regardless of gender, inherited the parental wealth, the couple decided that Malintzin would be traded to another tribe. It appears that Malintzin was traded several times and knew the cultural ways of many indigenous people.

Numerous works have been written on the conquest. Very briefly, in the 1500s, the Spanish European emerged on the continent for the purpose of exploring and claiming new land, acquiring silver and gold, and spreading the teachings of Christianity. To achieve these goals, they first had to conquer the mighty Mexica Empire, but they could not do it alone. Hernán Cortés led Spanish soldiers and thousands of Indians in the conquest. Prior to the emergence of the Spanish upon the continent, the Mayans heard a weeping woman. She sometimes cried out a warning that something terrible was about to emerge upon the land. The Mayans in Mexico are said to have retreated into the forests of Yucatan and escaped most of the brutality experienced by other Indians in Mexico. Moctezuma got word of the premonition. When the presence of Cortés's ships was recorded and messages were sent to Moctezuma, Moctezuma became gravely concerned. There emerged a debate in his court over whether their plumed serpent god, Quetzalcoatl, was returning or if the Spanish were merely greedy men wanting conquest and riches.

As the Spanish emerged on the land, the controversy escalated. The powerful Cortés was light skinned, as was the plumed serpent god, Quetzalcoatl. Some therefore thought that Cortés was Quetzalcoatl returning to his people at the time Cortés landed in Mexico in 1521. Moctezuma was in a quandary that continued too long. To ensure against all possibilities, he sent gifts to Cortés: many precious tapestries, gold and silver jewelry, and other valuable articles, like quetzal plums, the most precious Aztec possession, and he sent Malintzin, who was among twenty other women meant to provide services. Cortés did not receive these women in the same cultural context in which they were presented. Moctezuma offered them as a peace offering to provide communal services for his group of men, but Cortés had ideas of private property and so assigned each woman to a specific man under his command.

Malintzin was originally assigned not to Cortés but to another soldier who later told Cortés that she knew several indigenous languages and was learning to speak Castellan, the form of Spanish spoken by the men who were mostly from Extremedura, in Spain. Cortés, being the sophisticated military man that he was, took Malintzin for himself and used her to give geographical descriptions and directions, as well as to explain the ways of the land and its people.

Cortés had the woman baptized, and her Indian name was changed to Spanish. Malintzin was baptized Doña Marina. In Mexican history she become known as la malinche, the traitor, although originally Cortés was called the traitor. The indigenous people of Mexico called Cortés the malinche (traitor), because they never knew whether or not he would keep his word. As history progressed and was documented in the male-dominated tradition, it recorded Doña Marina as the traitor and rationalized that her services were crucial, making it possible for Cortés to conquer Mexico.

MYTH AND LEGEND

Malintzin rendered a valuable service, but Cortés also motivated several thousand Indian men and fueled various tribal animosities toward the Aztecs in conquering the mighty empire. With his horses, guns, and thousands of men, he finally achieved his brutal purpose. It is speculated that Malintzin was a slave and a woman with nowhere to go. Historically, women have been forced to live with violent men because of lack of options. Malintzin might have remained with Cortés, doing what was necessary to stay alive. Jewish women in German concentration camps during World War II were in similar situations and similarly get blamed for cooperating with the enemy. The lack of options is horrendously demeaning to women, and such women suffer much as a result.

According to Bernal Díaz del Castillo (1963), a member of the conquest, Malintzin was a gentle, loving spirit who forgave her mother and stepfather and asked Cortés to be lenient with them. She claimed that God had been very gracious in freeing her from the worship of idols and making her a Christian. This same god, she said, had given her a son by her lord and master Hernán Cortés; she also had a husband, Juan Jaramillo. She would rather serve her husband and Cortés than do anything in the world. That brainwashing had taken place is clear. Moreover, what happened to fundamental ethics and the theological beliefs of Catholicism? Malintzin could have been brainwashed; having been given away was so painful and confusing, and the need to survive was so great that she became resigned to Cortés's way of life and beliefs. She wanted to end oppression.

There is a point in the historical account of Malintzin where history leaves off and fantasy begins. It is reported that Cortés and Malintzin had a child, and when he had to return to Spain, he wanted to take his child with him. This hardly makes sense, for intercourse with Indians was considered sodomy; but perhaps baptized Indians were different. In any case, it still does not make sense, for according to Díaz, Cortés had a wife in Spain. (He also had a mistress to whom he had promised marriage in Cuba.)

It is said that Cortés returned to Spain and that he could not take Malintzin with him but did want to take their son with him. Rather than part from her son, Doña Marina is said to have drowned him. In order to understand why a mother would kill a child, one must question the assumption that all women love their offspring and want them to live. More germane to the plot is the Indian contention that humans have spirits and that when humans die, the spirit must also rest. The worst thing that could happen to an Indian was to die away from its own land. Malintzin knew that the Spaniards were strange men and that surely they must come from a strange place. Her son would certainly die in this faraway, foreign land, and then his spirit would never rest. Rather than have his spirit cast into eternal damnation, Malintzin committed the ultimate sacrifice—she drowned her child in order to keep his spirit in his own land and lay it to rest.

When Doña Marina died and went to heaven, God, Jesus, or Saint Peter (the occupant of this role depends on who is telling the story, but in every case it is a lone white male) would not allow her to enter until she returned with the soul(s) (the number varies with who is telling the story) of her drowned child. Doña Marina laments the fact that she cannot get into heaven. She wails as she wanders the river, its tributaries, and the ditches, seeking the soul of her own child, or of any children, so that she can pass it on as her own child's soul. It is at this point that she becomes known as la llorona. In a never-ending quest, she wails a frightening cry as she searches painfully throughout the Southwest suffering both physical and mental anguish.

This story embodies some of the most symbolic aspects of Chicano culture. La llorona is a female figure symbolizing the people, and the dispossession and reclamation of their homeland. People who have left their homeland, as the Aztecs did, or who lose control of it, as the Mexicans did, embark on an incredible voyage. In surviving to reclaim their homeland, Chicano people appear to have experienced transformation. Those who appreciate stories about such voyages usually think of the survivor as a hero. But because society does not attribute heroic deeds to women, it rarely thinks of the hero as female. In fact, it does the opposite: it produces negative images of women.

Sheros are female heroes or role models who are women. Both males and females need them but for different reasons. Women need them in order to stretch beyond their prescribed gender roles; males need them in order to learn to respect women and their contributions. Both genders need them to learn and teach values, ethics, and mores. Because of institutionalized sexism, heroines are believed to be rare in American culture, and because Chicanos have been Europeanized and Americanized, they have failed to recognize their own cultural heroine. They have learned, and teach, the Euro-American conquerors' version of a male-centered history and civilization.

Today la llorona is a spiritual, mythological figure. At the same time she is real because so many claim to have actually seen her. In keeping with Indian tradition, many Chicanos believe in the reality of spirits. Even some psychiatrists will admit that if one believes a thing is real, it becomes real, at least to the believer. In constructing such a reality, one not only possesses a cognitive notion of its existence, but one behaves as if it were real, giving to it material properties. The story of la llorona mixes history, fantasy, and spirituality and establishes the history and origin of Mexican Americans. She is a survivor, and survivors, especially those who retain their culture in spite of overwhelming odds, are heroines.

LA BRUJA

La llorona is said to be cunning. Although she searches for the soul of her child, she will grasp the soul of any one. She is determined to get into heaven and has gone beyond haunting rivers and ditches. She also haunts the forests, graveyards, dumps, railroad yards, and other such dark places. Some believe she is a bruja, a witch. Sometimes la llorona is an ugly, old, woman dressed in heavy black clothing; at other times she is a beautiful woman dressed in a flowing white gown. Some maintain that if one sees her beautiful face, she changes into a horse or a horse's skull; a goat or a goat's skull; or a decrepit old woman. She has been seen in several states, where she remains a woman not to be trusted: She is deviant enough even to try to cheat her way into heaven. The story has many messages, especially for Chicanas. It speaks primarily to the social implications of unwed motherhood and child killing. In contemporary interpretation, it speaks to the implications of premarital sex, birth (and death) control, and abortion, for la llorona never married. Her child, or children, were illegitimate. Some Chicanos of the Southwest believe that the Catholic Church views illegitimacy as a mortal sin. To a limited extent this contention is changing, but these deeds entail severe social and spiritual consequences.

Interestingly, only the women suffered the severe consequences of ostracism, scandalous talk, scornful treatment, and the penalty of hell in the afterlife. This story, however, also speaks to the worth of human life (especially male) among Chicanos, which is very high.

Many Chicanos do not make the connection between Doña Marina and la llorona. Those who do believe that the Christian god was angry at Doña Marina for having engaged in an illicit affair and for having conceived an illegitimate child. This interpretation is evidenced by refusing to let her into heaven. Her punishment was an eternal damnation, and this damnation is relentless, worse than hell. Hell is a definite place. Some feel that she was sent to la chingada (infinity) and that she will never retrieve the souls of her dead children. The idea of eternal damnation is actually an Indian concept that also exists in Roman Catholic theology. It may be that eternal and infinite are a matter of semantics. But having been cast into a place worse than hell, la chingada is especially insulting to Chicanos. La chingada is not in a downward direction; it is lateral, interminable. It is a mestizo concept that will make men fight if anyone has the nerve to wish them there and say it out loud.

In fact, many words and beliefs are so powerful that few dare to say them out loud. As mentioned earlier, some believe la llorona is a bruja (sorceress), a woman capable of evil. Chicanos do not like to talk about witches and witchcraft because white people will think they are stupid or superstitious. White culture has rendered the indigenous way of knowing and conceptualizing reality as bad, unscientific folklore. In an appropriate setting, however, these stories are told, and true feelings about the power of women are discussed in ways that have no white interpretation. Note that la llorona changes form. Not only does her name change as her situation changes, but she goes from being a real human being to being a spirit that does not go on to the other world, and yet she survives in spite of the pain.

LA CURANDERA AND LA VIRGEN

If la bruja is the bad woman, then la curandera is the good woman. Curanderas are knowledgeable in the healing arts. There are other healers among women: medicas (medics), sobadoras (massage therapists), herbalistas (herbalists), and parteras (midwives). Curanderismo is rooted in ancient indigenous culture. In its current form it is a blend of indigenous spirituality and Spanish Catholicism. As it has developed, it has taken a woman beyond the usual homemaker's role, but keeps her within the realm of the nurturing being.

Even la llorona remains true to the form of the abnegated mother. Malintzin would rather have eternal unrest than allow her son's spirit to wander. This story and the roles of curanderas and mothers have led to stereotyping Chicanas and the expectation that they exist to serve, protect, and nourish others. This stereotype has caused great distress for contemporary women who have absorbed some Anglo values of individuality and upward mobility. Until very recently, there have been few role models for young Chicanas who wanted to retain their culture and still succeed in a world they themselves defined.

La Virgen de Guadalupe, who is the Mexican Virgin Mary and the patron saint of Mexico, is the role model for women who want families. This woman, who goes to heaven, loves her family unconditionally. Since the Bible gives little attention to her life after delivering the infant Jesus, Chicanas are limited in ways of being. They surely do not want to be bad women, as Mary Magdalene is in the Bible.

The Virgin Mary was introduced to the Americas by the Spanish through stories, prayers, statues, and pictures. In her name Spanish males destroyed the beautiful temples to indigenous spirits and gods. They took temple material and constructed colonial churches to the Holy Mother. In "civilizing" and Christianizing the Indians, they emphasized the power of the Virgin and taught that women should model their lives on hers. Spanish males even used the virgin to prove that their one Christian god was stronger than indigenous gods. Sometimes the Indians believed the Spaniards. Often they only sought to appease them and pretended to worship the white male goddess. When indigenous deities were consistent with what the Spanish wanted them to believe, there was a cultural blending. From this cultural blending emerged la Virgen de Guadalupe, a brown-skinned, Indian-looking Virgin Mary, who appeared to the Indian Juan Diego on December 12, 1531, on the hilltop of Tepeyac, a place where indigenous Mexicanos worshiped the Nahuatl goddess, Tonantzin, known as the protector of pregnant women.

Even though the new virgin provided much of the basis on which the Spanish were able to Christianize and maintain colonization, la bruja was seen to be in alliance with the devil, the Spanish European god of the underworld. The vehicle for distributing this knowledge in the Americas was rooted in the church and its alliance with the crown. The power of the church was (and is) concentrated in the hands of men. Thus, women are in an adversarial power relationship to its policy.

THE DOUBLE STANDARD

Sexism was not an issue in the 1800s, when Mexico sought to liberate itself from Spain and later from France. During all this time, family reputation (which is the male's reputation) was also used to control women. Social stratification was based on race and class standing. Upper-class Spanish women born in Spain were isolated and sheltered. Those born in the Americas held the second position. Below them were women of Spanish and indigenous origin, followed by the indigenous and African (the Spanish brought slaves) women. I have no evidence of how the legend of la llorona manifested itself during this time, but it is known that she survived Spanish colonization, taking on some European aspects and is familiar to barrios across the United States today.

Perhaps a more sympathetic analysis is in order because little attention is given to the fact that Cortés was a willing party in this story. He had more power and influence than Malintzin. The social message of the story supports a double standard that warns women, not men, against illegitimate childbirth, premarital sex, or sex without marriage. In the narrative, Cortés drops out of sight and suffers no consequences for any of his deeds. Thus, the story gives strong support and prescription for both genders. It prescribes not only appropriate female behavior and relates the consequences of inappropriate behavior, but it also grants men certain undebatable privileges. There is no sensitivity for behavior dictated by the social circumstances of women living under the pressures of male domination. Male domination is further supported by the oppressing influence of the patriarchal church. Its doctrine evidences extreme social pressure exerted on women to stay well within a defined gender role.

In traditional culture, males are given entitlement because they are born males. One of those privileges includes not being questioned or confronted by women. Doña Marina tells Cortés that she does not want the child to go to Spain. She steps out of her prescribed gender role and is severely punished. It is interesting to note that it is not Cortés who exacts the punishment but a superior being, a white male. This fact more firmly plants fear for deviating from the prescribed gender role and fixes la Chicana into that role.

Another idea we should return to is that of homeland. To Chicanos remaining on or revisiting the homeland is important, both while alive and after death. Interestingly, Malintzin never leaves her homeland. She remains there as a spirit that is alive anywhere in the world where there is *raza*. La llorona is everywhere *raza* is located. In an ironic way she is the symbolic mother of the *mestizaje*, part indigenous and part Spanish-European people. Through her, Chicanos reclaim the homeland. This is an heroic, political act.

In the 1960s, Chicanos tried to reclaim Aztlan culturally, academically, and politically. They did so both symbolically and in some very real, material ways. Some went as far as arming themselves. There was talk about secession of the Southwest from the United States, and Aztlan emerged as the battle cry of the Chicano civil rights movement. The movement was not without its problems, however, one of which was sexism and racism.

Continuing with the legend of la llorona will lend some insight. Some people say la llorona will steal any child, kill it, and take its soul in an attempt to fool God and gain entrance into heaven. This version of the story tends to depict women as evil, cruel, cheating, and, in general, immoral and unethical. Men are also made to appear dishonest, disloyal, and sexually promiscuous, but implied in how the story is told is that it is the woman's fault. She bears responsibility for both herself and the male. The legend presents negative views of both males and females, but it uses women to scare children. It does, however, keep youth away from cemeteries, dangerous rivers, and irrigation ditches where they might drown. It also gets them home before dark and keeps their telephone use manageable.

La llorona can serve as a symbol of dignity, value, and worth. She is strong, human, and loving. She loves deeply and pragmatically when she will not allow Cortés to take their child, part Indian, to Spain. She kills her child to save his spirit from an indigenously prescribed eternal damnation, one she endured at the hands of the Catholic Spanish men who believed she murdered her son, a most atrocious crime for a woman.

In keeping with the idea that war and the violence of men have shaped the Chicana's life, we have to remember that Chicanas are descendants of the conqueror and of the conquered. They remain conquered on their homeland, and their status and power have changed minimally with changes in the politics of men at national and international levels. Raza has been symbolically vindicated by indigenous belief via a woman who was forced to interrelate with the conqueror. A strategy for decolonization is to permit women to share the leadership and for others to learn the coping mechanisms (linguistic, clothing, adornments, cooking, and spirituality) that Chicanas have developed to deal with oppression.

Unlike the contemporary stereotype of Chicanas and other Latinas, who symbolize sexual indiscretion and the triumph of Christianity, la llorona emerges scorned and castigated. Chicanos (males) have not modified this attitude. The story does not change much. When raza's circumstance changes, the story will change. For now, la llorona reclaims Aztlan and keeps alive the spirit of eternal struggle. The Chicana movement strove to overcome oppressive conditions, but it also sought to sustain the rich elements of the Chicano culture, highlighting female contributions. The problem, however, was male dominance and the culture's too frequent consistency with female oppression.

REFERENCES

Blea, Irene I. 1991. *La Chicana and the Intersection of Race, Class and Gender*. New York: Praeger.

Castillo, Ana. 1995. *Massacre of the Dreamers: Essays on Xicanisma*. Albuquerque: University of New Mexico Press.

Cotera, Martha. 1976. *Diosa y Hembra*. Austin, Tex.: Information Systems Development.

Díaz (del Castillo), Bernal. 1963. *The Conquest of New Spain*. Trans. J. M. Cohen. New York: Penguin Books.

Enriquez, Evangelina, and Alfredo Mirande. 1979. *La Chicana: The Mexican American Woman*. Chicago: University of Chicago Press.

Figueroa Torres, J. Jesus. 1975. *Doña Marina: Una India Ejemplar*. Mexico, D.F.: Ed. B. Costa-Amic.

Gomez-Tagle, Silvia, Adrian Garcia Valdes, and Lourdes Grobet. 1985. *National Museum of Anthropology: Mexico*. Trans. Joan Ingram-Eiser. Distribución Cultural Especializada.

Paz, Octavio. 1961. *Labyrinth of Solitude*. New York: Grove Press.

5

THE FEMINIZATION OF RACISM: CHALLENGING A COLONIAL LEGACY

Since there were roughly 30,000 women with various interests at the 1995 U.N. conference on women, it was difficult to assess how many Chicanas were present. The highlight of the NGO conference for about eleven of us was the panel on which I and three other Chicanas were scheduled to appear. It was difficult contacting one another at the hotels because of our inability to speak Chinese. In the end, various complications prevented the women who were supposed to be on my panel from appearing, and I had to go on alone. I arrived early, and one by one Chicanas approached asking if they had arrived at la Chicana panel after having searched for it among hundreds of other activities. The joy of meeting one another halfway across the world was a rite of passage for us.

The real highlight for the majority of attendees, however, came when Hillary Rodham Clinton and Winnie Mandela appeared. On the day that the U.S. First Lady was to speak, it rained and some commotion resulted when not everyone could get into the hall where she was to speak. South Africa's Mandela was five minutes late for her appointment and yet another commotion erupted when she complained that guards would not let her into her session. The two women were striking contrasts: the one very white, from one of the most powerful countries in the world, and the other black, from one of the poorest, most underdeveloped countries. The contrast forced me to continue to demand that racism be made a

Two comadres greet one another at a family wedding. Photograph by Oscar Castillo.

feminist issue. A delegation of the women of color met with the platform committee and by the end of the conference, racism had been feminized.

SURVIVING WAR

Chicanas have long felt that they are less than second-class citizens. They have felt the sting of being treated "like dogs," and being called breeding machines and welfare queens. Therefore, Chicanas identify more strongly with Third World women than with Anglo or white women in their own country. At the time the women were meeting in China, the war in Bosnia was receiving much attention, and in Chiapas, Mexico, indigenous peoples had rebelled against what they considered the source of their oppression, the Mexican government. Other countries in the Americas that have also experienced war recently are El Salvador and Guatemala. The hardships associated with these wars have motivated some migration to the United States. At the U.N. conference, Chicanas visited their sisters in the Latina tent where the Chicana's special sensitivity to societies characterized by war or ethnic struggle was much in evidence. A major issue at the conference was the need to redefine war crimes to include the rape and torture of women during times of war. Reports of both rape and torture were discussed throughout the conference grounds. Rape, especially during wartime, is a declaration of power, victory, and ownership. This process that defiles the opponent has traditionally been part of warfare. It can even be considered a celebration ritual associated with conquest. Women do not declare war and are not fully represented in world governments; they are therefore the innocent victims of war.

Except for immigrant women, contemporary U.S. women have not experienced warfare on their own soil. The War for Independence from Great Britain and the Civil War only conjure up romantic memories and far distant memories for most. For indigenous Americans and Chicanas, their war experience on their own homeland has cut into the fiber of their being because the ramifications of those wars persist. Whereas other U.S. women have had experiences with war during the two world wars as well as the Korean, Vietnam, and Gulf conflicts, Chicanas and other women of color face other wars in their country: those that are experienced in the streets, in business, in education, and in the nation's political offices.

The most fearsome element of the war for Chicanas is covered by the term *ethnic cleansing*, which emerged during the mid-1990s. Basically, this term means keeping the race pure. It is a frightening concept to those women who understand it. In the mid- and late 1800s, the white man's prevailing sentiment about Mexicans was to exterminate them as one would cockroaches.

War has been devastating to the Chicana. The older generation of Chicanas who lived through World War II went without the benefits of economic support for a college education, a credit rating, and health and hospital benefits. The next generation of women, those involved with the Vietnam War, saw their young brothers, boyfriends, and husbands killed and maimed, become drug addicted or alcoholic, go to prison, and commit suicide because of the unresolved psychological disturbances caused by the war. They lived with men who slept with knives and guns under their pillows at night and with men who took years to waste away because of Agent Orange. They raised children under these conditions, suffering poverty, emotional abuse, and physical and spiritual exhaustion. Yet, they and their children are not counted as part of the war casualties. Chicanas were especially burdened, because Chicano men were disproportionately represented in these wars. Moreover, the Chicana's people are the product of the rape and oppression that is part of the history of the country that is now theirs.

CONQUERED WOMEN

The Spanish conquest of Mexico in the mid-1500s significantly changed the lives of Indian women. Spanish colonialism extended geographically throughout the Americas as far north as Alaska. After the conquest, indigenous women who had once reigned as goddesses now wore the facial brands of slavery and were subjected to the imposition of a single male Christian god. By the time they arrived, Spanish women had already been well indoctrinated into male dominance. Early male colonialists explored and settled in Mexico and in the United States, but they also exerted their forceful presence in Guatemala, El Salvador, Ecuador, Peru, and Chile. Throughout Central and North America, they had contact with indigenous people. The period is broadly defined as the Spanish colonial period, and includes the exploration and settlement period after the conquest. Chicanas focus on events in Mexico because that country is closest to the Chicana experience physically, culturally, and spiritually.

Much of male history revolves around war, violent encounters, and land acquisition. In their own special way, women nurture those who survive and contribute to the social reconstruction that is needed after the trauma. U.S. Chicano men have documented their history in much the same pattern as Anglo men. They write about the outstanding accomplishments of men and about the violence they claim helped build the United States. They frequently accept historical periods as identified by the dominant culture's men, and they use the same paradigms for their analysis. Males doing Chicano Studies are a bit more skilled at questioning some of these constructs, but for the most part they, too, use them. Chicanas, who have been educated by men, often do the same because they are the products of an educational institution that conceptualizes and teaches history using white, male-dominated models of superiority. These models are hierarchical and categorical, and pose sharp dichotomies.

The conquistadors came to the Americas primarily from the area of Spain known as Extremedura. Pizzaro, who conquered Peru, was from Trujillo, and Cortés was from an area near Trujillo. These men and the armies that came with them arrived in the Americas without women. The Spanish male conquest of Mexico was followed by years of European colonialism, that introduced a new language, a new religion, new diseases, and a new way of looking at the world and its inhabitants. This new way especially demeaned women and demanded both male and female indigenous labor. Indian women worked in ore and mineral mines, and produced tallow for candles used in the rich mines; they also provided domestic and sexual services. Women worked in silk production, an old Chinese tradition, by harvesting silk worms taped beneath their breasts. They also worked in bakeries, in the sugar and chocolate mills, and in wineries. There, as workers, and in the homes of men as wives and maids, they were a source of information and companionship to men. They rarely involved themselves with Spanish men voluntarily. Some of them were given or traded to upper-class Spanish men by lower-class Indian men in order to preserve the saliency of Indian households.

From time to time, indigenous culture was integrated into Spanish culture, but generally gods and goddesses of the earth, the underworld, and the heavens were replaced with concepts symbolized by the male-dominated Catholic Church: by God the father; Jesus His son; Mary the earthly virgin mother; and the devil. To encourage conversion to Catholicism, indigenous holidays were observed using Christian deities. By 1572, the Catholic friars are reported to have baptized, confirmed, and married most, if not all, of Mexico. Cotera (1976) notes that after the conquest thousands of women had their faces deformed by branding, which was customary in order to traffic women through the slave market. Married and single women were taken at will.

Except for Queen Isabella, there is little mention of the women Spanish men left behind and of those who later came to the New World. We know a little about the elite women of Spain by studying Queen Isabella, who was part of the monarchy that lavished a huge portion of the Americas' gold to arrest the spread of Protestant heresies in Western Europe. From her lineage we gain insights into the complex family structure of that period as well as the arranged marriages and gender roles among the most powerful. Not all of this history is pleasant. It is a well-established fact that Isabella sponsored Christopher Columbus's voyage to the Indies, which turned out to be the Americas. She was more interested in overseas exploration than her husband, Ferdinand. Isabella and Ferdinand were known as the Catholic monarchy, a title conferred upon them by Pope Alexander VI. The couple negotiated brilliant deals, including their own marriage and the alliances of their four children. Their eldest daughter was the Infanta Isabella, who married the crown prince of Portugal; the Infanta Catherine of Aragon became the first wife of England's Henry VIII; and the Infanta Juana and her brother, Don Juan, heir to the throne, respectively, married Archduke Philip and Archduchess Margaret, son and daughter of Maximilian von Habsburg, the Holy Roman Emperor. Don Juan and la Infanta Isabella died young, leaving children who died in infancy. Catherine failed to produce an heir to Henry the VIII and became the injured party of the world's most notorious divorce case. Juana married at age sixteen and soon began to show signs of mental illness. To make matters worse for her, Philip was unfaithful. Through her mother, Isabella, Juana was heiress to the crown of Castile, whose laws forbade the succession of the Aragonese Ferdinand. Before Isabella died in 1504, she willed a provision that Ferdinand should act as regent if "Juana la Loca" (the crazy) proved unable to govern. The following year, Ferdinand attempted to assume the regency, but his son-in-law aborted this move and stepped in to assume the Castillian crown as Philip I. Philip died a few months later, and Juana, as characterized by myth and gossip, lived in forced seclusion. Ferdinand ruled over her dominions until he died in 1516, at which time Charles, the eldest of Juana la Loca and Philip I's five children, assumed the throne of Spain.

Isabella and Ferdinand were first cousins. It was not unusual for first cousins to marry; even today many Chicanas have been raised in families where cousins marry each other. During the lifetimes of Isabella and Ferdinand, it was also not unusual for men, often widowed, to marry several times. Women married young, at the age of thirteen and fourteen. If they did not die in childbirth, they often became sickly. They were under great pressure to produce male heirs.

Early in the explorations of the Americas, the Spanish conquistador wives, mothers, and daughters remained in Spain to oversee households and plots of land and to continue with various forms of business. Some women chose to live together on larger estates. While married women remained in Spain, the men frequently forgot they were married. Few women, however, likely forgot their nuptial vows, because of the female's place in Spanish society and because of the heavy influence of the Catholic faith. Our contemporary jokes about chastity belts are a cultural remnant of those times.

What was happening to the women in Spain during this time? Spanish women with families would not come to the New World until Queen Isabella (La Católica) intervened. She set forth a number of decrees guiding the moral behavior of Spanish men in New Spain, one of which stated that no men without families, unless they were priests, were allowed to venture to the New World (Cotera, 1976). Reports of atrocities committed against the indigenous populations, especially against Indian women, seriously concerned the queen. Proclaiming that only priests and men with families be allowed to come to the hemisphere was her way of addressing the matter of atrocities.

WOMEN DURING THE COLONIAL PERIOD

The Spanish were in the area now known as the United States as early as 1528. The first recorded expedition was Cabeza de Vaca's shipwreck near Galveston, Texas. By 1539, the Spaniards had explored as far north as central New Mexico. Fray Marcos and the black Arab, Estevan, journeyed through Sonora into Arizona and the Zuni villages. In 1540, Francisco Vásquez de Coronado organized his expedition and went into what is now the United States. Rodriguez Cabrillo explored the San Diego Bay in 1542. In 1769 Fray Junipero Serra settled San Diego. History has not taught us, however, that the first European women came to the Southwest with some of these Spanish expeditions. They traveled with Spaniards, indigenous, and mestizos. One woman on Juan Bautista de Anza's expedition gave birth to a child on the way to California in 1575 (Cotera, 1976). In May 1598, Juan de Onate, the husband of the granddaughter of Cortés and great-granddaughter of Moctezuma (Mirande and Enriquez, 1979), guided 210 people from Zacatecas to San Juan de los Caballeros, near Santa Fe, New Mexico. The troop included men, women, children, servants, and household goods. Only forty of the original 210 stayed in New Mexico. From 1603 to 1680, small groups of soldiers with and without families joined the original settlers. Most scholars drop the indigenous story here and proceed with the European or Anglo settlement narrative, but the Indian women taught the priests (women and children were closest to the mission structure) and early colonials many things about living on the land. How much indigenous women taught the Spanish woman in whose homes they worked is unknown, but no doubt it was a significant amount. Indigenous women taught Spanish women how to produce finishes on the adobe walls of houses with their bare hands. They also built outdoor *hornos* (ovens), dehydrated food for storage, and developed a new cuisine.

Culturally and genetically, much exchange took place between the Anglos and the native populations. During the early period there was much intermarriage, so much so that the early Chicano scholar Cary McWilliams (1968) thought the indigenous population should be regarded as part of the Chicano population. The populations share racial background, language, childbearing patterns, social relationships with Anglos, and often the Catholic religion. Some indigenous people and Chicanos have resisted McWilliams' suggestion. Thus far, a meaningful dialogue on the subject has not taken place. Indeed, as McWilliams proposed, Chicanas and Chicanos should probably be considered part of the indigenous population.

Spanish activity between 1528 and 1608 produced missions, *presidios* (military compounds), and civilian colonies. The Spanish incorporated some indigenous customs and introduced various fruits, animals, Spanish architecture, irrigation techniques, and laws, ranching, and cowboy traditions to the indigenous. Women adopted the indigenous ways of cleaning, health, healing, and spiritual approaches. Many of these bicultural practices remain alive today throughout the Southwest. The colonial period in both Mexico and what is now the U.S. Southwest was not conducive to the development of increased status for women. Its forces were employed to maintain women's roles of submission as daughters and wives. There were few other roles for women. The colonial period was also not conducive to the well-being of the indigenous. In the United States much conflict occurred, and both indigenous and Spanish took slaves or servants. In 1680, New Mexico's indigenous population revolted against the Spanish, who were forced to flee to Isletta, a place near El Paso.

One of the greatest literary figures of this period was the so-called tenth muse, Sor Juana Ines de la Cruz, who entered a convent in order to study. Sor Juana Ines de la Cruz was the first woman in the Americas to openly question male domination, especially in the Catholic Church. Details of her life remain controversial. For example some say she was born a Criolla, whereas other maintain she was an Española. Some (Cotera, 1976) contend that she was born in 1648 and others (Enriquez and Mirande, 1979) claim 1651. It is known, however, that she continued to produce written works into the 1690s and that she was placed in school at the age of three. By the age of eight she was writing plays and poetry. She advanced far beyond the expectations of a cloistered nun. From her physically comfortable but socially conflicted life, we learn that women were not allowed to engage in advance studies. That is why her mother cut de la Cruz's hair and allowed her to dress in boys' clothing. De la Cruz incorporated various areas of knowledge and science into her writings. To Chicanas and the world at large, she represents a highly sophisticated, intellectual feminist. Among her writings are *Las Redondillas*, a collection of poems dealing with male-female issues, and *Contra la Injusticias de Hombre al Hablar de la Mujer* (Against the Injustices of Men's Attitudes in Talking About Women).

Other women of this period worthy of mention included the social activists Sor Felipe de Jesus, Sor Antonio Perez de los Santos, Sor Rosa, Sor Antonio de la Santisima Trenidad, and Rosa de Loreto, all of whom were indigenous women who converted to Catholicism and attended the Convento de Corpus Christi. Sor Juana, like de la Cruz, entered the convent in order to study; a religious life was secondary to her love of learning. Her natural intelligence led her to write essays, letters, and entire theological theses about the Catholic Church, its theology, its male dominance, and the nature of gender relations in the general society. Her feminist perspective on men and the church cost her dearly. The clergy made strenuous efforts to get her to conform to the church hierarchy, and in the end they took away her books and scientific equipment. Sor Juana tried to conform, but, within two years of displacement from her studies, she died. Sor Juana is the first feminist in the Western Hemisphere.

Until the U.S. war with Mexico in 1848, women were relatively freer on the frontier than in the cities. As the Spanish ventured into what is now the U.S. Southwest, they found indigenous social structures similar to those they had encountered earlier in Mexico but on a different scale. Western pueblos were subdivided into matrilineages and grouped into clans, where women had important functions at home and on the land and cared for ceremonial, or religious, articles (Swadesh, 1974).

THE HERITAGE OF INDEPENDENCE

Women of the Americas, like Chicanas, have encountered fundamental contradictions by demanding independence from eurocentric oppressive governments and patriarchy. In 1810, during Mexico's war of independence from Spain, Gertrudis Bocanegra, a woman from a respected family, organized an effort to educate the Indians. The government felt not only that her actions were unfeminine and unbecoming for a person of her class, but also that they threatened the government because if Indians learned to read and write, they might revolt. In Bocanegra's time, some indigenous women were allowed to remain in their families under Spanish rule. These families were to provide administrative services and structures for the new rulers. The devaluation of the Indian female's status is seen until the 1700s, when the mighty Cacique (indigenous rulers) lines were weakened. The population served menial roles as artisans, storekeepers, and farmers, and during this period the indigenous woman's role grew even weaker with the construction of convents to house them apart from Españolas (Spanish women).

U.S. Chicanas have modeled their lives after Sor Juana Ines de la Cruz and women like Gertrudis Bocanegra, who was active in the year of El Grito de Delores (the cry for Mexican independence). Bocanegra organized small underground armies of women who smuggled supplies into the battlefield. She was taken prisoner, questioned and tortured, and on October 17, 1817, she was executed for not cooperating with supporters of the status quo. Like many other women, her activities and contributions went unrecognized for nearly 120 years.

The war of independence from Spain cannot be discussed without including Josefa Ortíz de Dominquez, known as La Corregidora, a criolla of Querataro. During the war, women performed many heroic deeds and were not exempt from prison and execution. Dominguez identified strongly with the poor and the indigenous, even though she was from the elite class. She had spent part of her childhood in one of Mexico's orphanages. Through her daughter's suitors she met Cura Miguel Hidalgo y Costilla, famous for the grito, the cry, that began the war. Dominguez was a supporter of the liberation movement and was imprisoned several times for her political activities. From prison she communicated with the rebels until her release in 1820. To the very end of her life she refused recognition awards and maintained that her struggle was not against Spain but against those who had oppressed her people. Dominguez was completely estranged from her family because of her activities.

Other women of interest from the same period are María Fermina Rivera and Manuela Medina, La Capitana (the captain), who fought in battles; and Luisa Martinez, who like Bocanegra was ultimately executed. The list is extensive and includes Rafaela Lopez Aguado de Rayon from Michoacan; Ana García Francisca y Magdalena Goda, from Coscomaltepec; María Tomasa Estevez y Solas, from the Villa de Salamanca; Antonio Nova y Catalina Gonzales, from Sierra de Xaliaca; Dolores de Catalan, María del Socarro Díaz, María Ocampo, Loreto Encina de Aviles, Patricia Villalobos, and Soledad Solorzano de Regules (Cotera, 1976).

After liberation from the crown, the former New Spain became Mexico, which extended into what is now known as the U.S. Southwest. The U.S. war with Mexico ended Mexican domination there. This time of conflict, violence, and extraordinarily hostile warfare created the U.S.–Mexican border and ceded to the United States the five southwestern states of Texas, Arizona, New Mexico, Colorado, and California, as well as parts of Nevada. Contemporary Chicanas identify strongly with the state in which they live. More resistant and culturally nationalist Chicanas refer to the entire area as Aztlan, or occupied Mexico. The U.S. border is still an area characterized by conflict, and armed officials of both countries patrol it. At the border, the current drug war is about keeping drugs out of the United States; but a war has also been declared against allowing Mexicans into the United States without documentation. This imaginary line is a focal point for much controversy, killings, and searches of persons and property. We must remember, however, that men created this line and other lines on maps.

The Southwest region was settled by Spanish colonial families, which included a good number of women. As Solome Hernández (1986) points out, male leaders could not have succeeded without the help of the sel-dom-mentioned indigenous and Spanish females who were their ser-vants, wives, and sisters. Little record is left of these women. In Espejo's early expedition to New Mexico in 1582, Miguel Sánchez Valenciano was accompanied by his wife, Casilda de Amaya, and their three sons. We know little else other than she was pregnant during the long journey across the desert. During this period, the Spanish took indigenous women who fought for their lives, plotted escapes, and died.

Women also accompanied Juan de Onate into New Mexico in 1598. Listed among the colonists were forty-seven wives, and an Indian woman with a Spanish name and the respectful title of doña. She is simply known as Doña Inez. Wives more frequently traveled with their officer husbands than they did with ordinary soldiers. Many of these women were left widows. A list of women and servants from the 1600s who came as travelers with a replacement garrison troop names eight Spanish women and thirteen servants. Among the servants was Isabel de Olvera, who feared harassment because she was mulatto (mixed blood). She gave a deposition to the royal officials declaring that she was a free woman, unmarried, and the legitimate daughter of Hernando, a Negro male, and an indigenous woman named Magdalena.

A few other scattered facts are recorded about women in the 1600s. Stories about the Lady in Blue (believed to be the Virgin Mary) circulated among the indigenous. In 1629, some newly arrived friars declared that it was common understanding that a nun named María de Jesus de la Concepcion, of the Order of Saint Francis, was miraculously transported to New Mexico to preach the Catholic faith.

During this period, women in Spain were not allowed to speak or write in the public sphere. In 1680, ninety years after the initial Spanish settlement, the pueblo people revolted in New Mexico. That year 1,795 men and women fled the area and walked to Isleta, near El Paso, Texas, taking only 20 carts with them. Many women were also killed during the revolt; among them Francisca Domínguez, who lay naked, her head crushed. A lance thrust into her head emerged from her throat. A child at her feet looked as though it had been aborted (Hernández, 1986). Some of the women were captured and were forced to live with their captors. Others were rescued twelve years later, along with "half-breed" children they had given birth to during their captivity. Among those reunited in 1692 were Petrona Pacheco and her three children, plus María Naranjo, Juana Hurtado, and Juana de Apodaca.

Individuals and families were allowed to go to the provincial frontier only by permission of the crown. The early settlers lived with established policies. Women worked in the fields, managed ranches, bore children, and raised, clothed, and educated them. They relied on food, herbs, mas-sage, and prayers for health and healing. Some had as many as thirteen living children, many of whom died. Women built houses, planted, nursed the sick, and took care of livestock. When an area had a church, they cleaned it, plastered its walls, cared for the priests, prepared the altar, helped establish religious organizations, and gave religious instruction. Some could read and write in Spanish.

Veyna (1986) has carefully surveyed notarial documents from Santa Fe and Santa Cruz de la Canada in New Mexico. The records she reviews cover the years 1710–1733, over one hundred years before the signing of the Treaty of Guadalupe Hidalgo and the admission of the U.S. Southwest into the union. Women had more presence in the courts, a public facility. They bought and sold various personal and landed property, recorded wills, and provided testimonials. This activity diminished after 1848, and women's presence became minimal.

During the Mexican period, 1810–1848, Spanish was spoken and some traditions continued. Social conflict continued between the Mexicans and indigenous until the Americans arrived. One of the most glamorous of the frontier women was Doña Tules, Gertrudis Barcelo. Barcelo owned a saloon and gambling house, La Tules, where she entertained influential Mexicanos and Americanos with dancing, drinking, and card games. Her establishment became a central meeting place that she used to finance politicians when necessary. She was an accomplished Monte (card) dealer who smoked, was independent, and respected. This enterprising and industrious businesswoman also did charity work for the church and took in orphans. In 1850, she wrote a will documenting that she had extensive property and other resources that she declared had been accumulated through her own labor and exertions. From her life we gain some indication of women's roles in transition (Hernández, 1986) from Mexican patriarchy to American patriarchy. This transition was hostile to women and can be witnessed in the comments of Mexican women as reproduced in the work of Genaro M. Padilla (1993).

Apparently, women attained higher status and relative freedom on the frontier. This was primarily a response to severe conditions; but Frances Leon Swadesh (1974) believes that it may also have been a result of early male intermarriage with the Pueblo women, whose culture warranted giving them more social flexibility. Unsupervised women and girls infrequently herded livestock in distant pastures. They routinely cared for livestock grazing in *dehesas* (community irrigated pastures). Men frequently did their work without the presence of women. They did their own cooking in sheep camps, on long buffalo hunts, and on trading journeys. While they were gone, women and children frequently ran the farms and ranches.

Mestizo and indigenous women butchered and treated the skins of animals. They irrigated the fields and harvested crops. Some elderly and some wealthy women were specialists in crafts, herbal medicine, and midwifery. The term *doña* was reserved for elderly and wealthy women. Women who practiced the healing arts as curanderas and medicas (general healers), sobadoras (massage therapists), parteras (midwives), and herbalistas (herbalists) were most important. Many a rancher and farmer rode his horse or walked many miles to bring the medicine woman with her healing specialty to his family.

As urban centers developed, not all the frontier women lived on ranches and farms. Some of them went to work or lived in nearby towns. They worked in hotels as maids, in laundries, and in restaurants. There were even a few prostitutes in the now well-established cities of Santa Fe, Tucson, Los Angeles, and San Antonio.

THE U.S. WAR WITH MEXICO

In the United States mestizos and indios (indigenous) were conquered by members of the Anglo-centered culture. After three hundred years, Chicanas became conquered women on their own land, thus occupying the lowest rung of the social ladder. Political conflict became race/ethnic conflict. Today the conflict continues in the form of policies such as English as the official language of the United States, Propositions 187 and 209 in California. Proposition 187 limits social services to undocumented workers, and 209 does away with affirmative action ensuring equal treatment in the labor market. Even the use of language is a battle. For example, Chicanas do not refer to the Mexican-American War as such. They proclaim that the war was provoked by the United States. Therefore, it more rightly was the U.S. war with Mexico. The use of language is the Chicana's way of protesting the aggrandizment of Anglo accomplishments and is a move to correct history. It is an effort to make people more reality based. Their reality is that the United States occupied the Southwest. The Southwest, together with its native and Spanish-speaking population, was colonized as a result of Anglo greed and cravings for expansion (Acuna, 1988). Thus, Chicanas live in occupied territory.

A very small minority opinion contends that the war ended in 1848 and that Chicanas are therefore U.S. citizens with full U.S. privileges. Members of this group minimize the existence of racism and note the upward mobility of selected individuals. Those opposed to this perspective note that individual mobility has not translated into group mobility and cultural respect.

The involuntary incorporation of the Chicanos into the United States was the result of an international treaty, the Treaty of Guadalupe Hidalgo, signed on February 2, 1848. The treaty has been very controversial and the basis of Chicano resistance to assimilation. It not only made Mexicanas Americans, but it also outlined the rights and privileges of former Mexican citizens without giving attention to gender or to the fact that the people it had just incorporated into its new borders were, in part, inherent to the land. Native people did not become official citizens of the United States until the early 1900s.

During the U.S. war with Mexico, Mexico was in no shape to defend itself from Anglo imposition. It had struggled for its own independence from Spain and from France, and was weak in its own northernmost territory. The war was characterized by racism and hatred on both sides. The American sexist and racist expansionist mentality manifested itself in reactions to the conditions the Mexican government had imposed in order to allow Americans to live in northern Mexico. Americans failed to comply with the conditions, which included obeying Mexican law and practicing Catholicism. Southerners were especially irate about the abolition of slavery in Mexico. They needed land and wanted to keep their slaves. Conspiracy was in the interest of both U.S. northerners and southerners. The aim was to annex Mexico's northern territory, acquire its gold, silver, and other minerals, and expand the capitalist economy (Acuna, 1988).

Many Mexicans lost their lives in the struggle with the United States. One-half of Mexico's total territory was ceded to the United States, which thereby acquired a population ranging from 80,000 to 350,000; exact numbers remain obscure. The indigenous kept the Anglos from effectively colonizing the territory for another forty years, but even that battle was lost and the reservation system was established.

During and shortly after this period, arranged intermarriage was common between Spanish women and Anglo men. Before the Anglo conquest, it was a primary way for Anglo men to become Mexican citizens and obtain Mexican land. After the war, the practice was necessary in order to allow landed Mexicans to retain their land holdings.

Anglo colonization posed more immediate hardships for Mexicanas from families with little or no land base. Cotera (1976) draws attention to Doña Patricia de Leon (1795–1849), one of the founders of Victoria, Texas, who amassed a great fortune in land. Her story is the story of many upper-class Mexican families who cooperated with the Anglos. Prior to the war, Doña Patricia and her husband established good relations with the president of Mexico and secured a large land grant. They developed the land, using the inheritance brought into the marriage by Doña Patricia. The family collaborated with the Anglo forces during the war, and in the end they were not trusted by the Mexicans and were rejected by Anglos. They were forced to flee to Louisiana where they lived in poverty for some time, until Doña Patricia went to Mexico and then returned to Victoria, Texas.

Chicano rights as new U.S. citizens were well defined in the Treaty of Guadalupe Hidalgo, which granted them U.S. citizenship, with full rights and responsibilities. After the war, land grabbing and defamation of the Spanish and mestizo language and culture became the order of the day. A dual economy complete with a dual wage system developed (Barrera, 1979; Blea, 1988), one for Anglos and another for Mexicans evolved. Mexicanos were excluded from equal education. Their schools, books, and teachers were all inferior. Political participation, especially for women, was impossible, and they lost their land through legal definitions, decisions, and taxes that favored the Anglo. Chicanos also suffered religious discrimination, shootings, hangings, and general violence. Many women were raped and otherwise violated. Both males and females resisted, but none of this was recorded in the U.S. history books.

Women saw their men being defined as social bandits (Acuna, 1988; Blea, 1988; Mirande, 1985) defending their land and the honor of Mexicanas. Social banditry is a process whereby Anglo media and attitudes made those who resisted oppression appear as bad people and as persons whom Mexicans should be ashamed of. Chicano and Anglo historians both elected to depict the experiences of men during this time, but ignored the attitudes and experiences of women until women began to demand more accurate scholarship.

Women have always been perceived and treated as part of the spoils of war. Thus it was that white men felt free to impose on Mexican women after the war. Before, during, and after the war many Mexican women experienced rape, loss of land, and other resources, culminating in a severe deterioration in their quality of life. Both men and women were harassed, falsely accused of wrongdoing, and lynched. In fact, the first recorded lynching of a woman took place in Downieville, California, on July 5, the day after U.S. Independence Day, in 1851 (Cotera, 1976), only three years after the American conquest. The story told about Josefa Segovia is distorted, but it appears that the lynching enraged the people so deeply that violence broke out among the men. There is disagreement about her marital status. Some contend that Josefa was a prostitute, but Rodolfo Acuna (1988) claims that she was not.

Josefa was a Sonoran and was of good character, above the average of camp women of those days. She lived in a shack with a gambler named Manuel Jose and was about twenty-six years old, petite, with large dark eyes that at times flashed, like a devil, as one white observer reported. During a drunken rage, one of the white miners broke down Josefa's door. When Jose found out and approached the miner about it away from the house, the miner accused Josefa of being a prostitute. An argument ensued. Josefa got involved in the argument, and the white man called her a prostitute and other vile names. Josefa said, "This is no place to call me bad names, come into my house and call me that." The white man did just that, and Josefa killed him by stabbing him with a knife. The white miners wanted to lynch Josefa and Jose, but had to wait to achieve this purpose pending the results of a trial. Even though the defense revealed that Josefa was pregnant, she was lynched. It is estimated that over 2,000 men lined the river to watch her hang at the bridge. Most male scholars contend that Josefa has no recorded last name, implying she had no family origin and cannot be genetically traced to a man. If she had not been the first woman hanged in the United States, she would have no importance to American history. Martha Cotera, however, informed Chicano scholars in 1976 that her last name was Segovia.

Josefa was not married. Lifestyle options for women in mining camps were limited to wife or prostitute (i.e., good woman or bad woman). Women who were not aligned with men or were living with men but were not married had bad reputations. In short, women were categorized according to whether their sexual activity was sanctioned or unsanctioned. Josefa's need to save face forced her to invite the white man into the house in order to keep others from hearing the foul names he was calling her. We don't know what happened to Jose in the house, but this account suggests the frustrations of race relations, and how the legal system was often used to disproportionately punish Mexicans. We know that men used violence to deal with the conflict and that using pregnancy as a defense and a reason for leniency was not respected. Was there no need for any more Mexicans in California? Could it be that she was not pregnant? Did Mexican men identify more with the male victim than with Josefa? It appears that they and the white men both lined the river to watch Josefa be lynched. We get no information about the presence of other women. Could it be that Josefa suffered from the sexism of social banditry? One thing is clear: women have long struggled in wars of independence and in personal causes to liberate themselves from oppression in ways that have been masked by male dominance.

REFERENCES

Acuna, Rodolfo. 1988. *Occupied America: A History of Chicanos*. 3rd ed. New York: Harper and Row.

Barrera, Mario. 1979. *Race and Class in the Southwest*. Notre Dame, Ind.: University of Notre Dame Press.

Blea, Irene I. 1988. *Toward a Chicano Social Science*. New York: Praeger.

Cotera, Martha. 1976. *Diosa y Hembra*. Austin, Tex.: Information Systems Development.

Enriquez, Evangelina, and Alfredo Mirande. 1979. *La Chicana: The Mexican American Woman*. Chicago: University of Chicago Press.

Hernández, Solome. 1986. "Nueva Mexicanas as Refugees and Reconquest Settlers, 1680–1696." In Joan M. Jensen and Darlis A Miller, eds., *New Mexico Women: Intercultural Perspectives*. Albuquerque: University of New Mexico Press.

McWilliams, Carey. 1968. *North from Mexico: The Spanish-Speaking People of the United States.* New York: Greenwood Press. (Originally printed in 1949.)

Mirande, Alfredo. 1985. *The Chicano Experience.* Notre Dame, Ind.: University of Notre Dame Press.

Padilla, Genaro M. 1993. *My History, Not Yours: The Formation of Mexican American Autobiography.* La Cross: University of Wisconsin Press.

Swadesh, Frances Leon. 1974. *Los Primeros Pobladores.* South Bend, Ind.: University of Notre Dame Press.

Veyna, Angelina F. 1986. "Women in Early New Mexico: A Preliminary View." In T. Cordova et al., eds., *Chicana Voices: Intersections of Class, Race and Gender.* Austin: CMAS Publications, University of Texas Press.

6

EXISTING IN A STATE OF COLONIALIZATION

Chicanas are not the only persons sensitive to the suffering of women during war. At the 1995 U.N. conference of women, Japan apologized to the women of China for the past oppression Japan had imposed on them. Most of the women there understood the importance of apology, of "saving face," and of making atonement to women of color. Like the Chinese and the Japanese, Chicanas also need to hear an apology from the United States for the past wrongs it has imposed on her people. "Saving face" is nothing more than the cultural need to restore respect and good faith. It is a matter of dignity, self-worth, and justice. It is as important to Chicanas as apology and atonement are for the Japanese Americans relocated and incarcerated during World War II and for the Japanese bombed in Hiroshima and Nagasaki. These are not important social, political, and environmental concerns for those who do the victimizing, however. This lack of recognition and validation of cultural needs only feeds negative race relations.

LIVING WITH A DOMINANT CULTURE

Living with a dominant culture consists of balancing two very powerful cultures. Chicanas have a strong positive emotional tie to their culture, but the other culture is both feared and necessary. One culture nourishes, while the other threatens and even hurts. One allows a certain

Argentine-born actress Carmen Zapata and Margaritta Galban are just two of the many Latinas who have worked to empower the Chicano/Latino community. Photograph by Oscar Castillo.

comfort level, and the other discomfort. One is to be trusted; the other distrusted. The Chicana has no choice but to learn the dominant culture; it is a matter of survival, a fundamental need to know what the other assumes. For the Chicana, there are situational ethics in that other culture and basic understandings about how to talk, eat, and walk. It is obvious to the Chicana that among her own people she is beautiful, or she comes closer to the standard of beauty. In the other she cannot compete or be safe.

To Chicanas, living within a dominant culture means growing up knowing that their people lost the war and that the victors wrote their history to glorify themselves. La Chicana knows that her men, as well as some of her women, have been hanged, wrongfully charged, incarcerated, and robbed. She knows that discrimination is real, that segregation is real; and she knows that under the U.S. law, this was legal for a long time. Even now, she knows that it takes place and that few want to believe it. Living in a dominant culture is to live with contradiction: knowing there are dual standards of justice, pay, education, and facilities. The contradiction is that the United States is supposed to be the land of freedom and justice for all. It is the land of equality. In contrast, the Chicana's life is divided in two, and she belongs to the least valued world.

Living in a dual culture is about not being able to be your self because half of the time you do not know who you are. The Chicano or Latino side is so strong and meets many needs, but it lacks so much power and resources that sometimes Chicanas are ashamed of who they are: Latinas. And if they are not ashamed, they are frustrated or angry, angry that what has happened to their people has happened in the richest, most powerful country in the world. They have been betrayed. They have obeyed all the rules. They have gone to school, learned the language, and worked hard. But the American Dream has not been for them. Nor has it been for Puerto Ricans, African Americans, Asians, and Native Americans. Freedom is relative to the relationship to the dominant culture and to money. In a country that boasts about being the most democratic in the world, democracy is categorical and hierarchically structured.

Ironically, social forces have blamed Chicanos for their social, economic, and political condition, and have tried to force la Chicana always to be representative of all her people, and to be ashamed enough of her culture, her poverty, and her people to give them up, but she has not. Thus, these same social forces keep her in a vise, squeezing her between two cultures. How she sustains herself is a mystery; surely, this is an area in need of much research. She does so by holding onto her sense of space (spiritual, physical, political, social), but she recognizes her reality and does not deceive herself about it, making a plan and following it through. If she does not, teen pregnancy devours her life; domestic abuse, sexism, racism, the Catholic Church, family, men, children, and unsafe streets are all ready to define her life for her.

Most of the problems listed above have been shared by other women around the world, but they have not been experienced as la Chicana has experienced them. Each woman lives her reality within a cultural context and in relationship to the dominant culture. Many women are members of the dominant culture and have little first-hand knowledge of the oppressed because they do not need this knowledge. The oppressed, on the other hand, must know the oppressor. Sometimes the oppressor is known so well and is reflected in such a positive light that the oppressed want to be like the oppressor. Sometimes the oppressed study the oppressor so well that they learn how to be like the oppressor. They lighten their skin, bleach their hair, and change their way of dressing, walking, and talking in order to belong. Sometimes they marry marginal members of the dominant group and have children, and they are happy.

For some Chicanas, resisting the oppressor has involved not acting, dressing, or speaking like them. For others, it has been to identify with the Mexican side, and not the indigenous side of them. For still others, it has meant being more Indian, accenting those traits that distinguish them from all oppressors. Yet, others do not want anything to do with downtrodden people. They claim the full privileges of U.S. citizenship. Eventually, they recognize that it is difficult, especially if they look Latino or Indian. In summary, living within the context of the dominant culture is extremely difficult and calls for the resolution of identity. The difficulty lies in the fact that racism and sexism change with the times and that women, especially Chicanas, need to redefine themselves with the ever changing forms of racism and sexism.

CHICANAS AS AMERICANAS

After the U.S. war with Mexico, strict social divisions were seen among Chicanos. Female and male labor were distinct, and class divisions intensified. Some women lived on very large estates and gained some privilege based on their sexual relationship to the estate owner, *el patron*. But most women worked on estates as the wives and daughters of *el peon*, the hired hand. Other women worked on small land parcels as wives or daughters of farmers. The number of women without husbands increased, as did the number of widows and poverty among women with families. Some of the large Spanish, and later Mexican, land grants had been granted directly to women like Doña María del Carmen Calvillo. Other women managed ranches they had inherited from husbands or fathers (National Women's History Project, 1992).

The Anglo invasion of Mexico and the signing of the Treaty of Guadalupe Hidalgo created Chicanas—colonized women who lived in a political state much as indigenous people living under a foreign government after being over taken in war. Since that time, Chicanas have joined their male counterparts in resisting the influence of Anglo colonization, which has both physical and psychological dimensions. For example, Chicanas have been stigmatized by their color, body type, and culture as lacking value. Psychologically, this stigma produces attitudes and behaviors of inferiority, especially when their spiritual practices are ridiculed and physical and social boundaries are set into place. Chicanos and Anglos have therefore been kept apart, separated by real and perceived differences, isolated from one another.

After the Mexican War, the Catholic Church cooperated with the new government. The central seat of the church was moved from Durango, Mexico, to St. Louis, Missouri. Euro-American-style churches replaced mission architecture. The Church replaced leading Mexican officials with non-Mexican officials, and eventually brought in euro-identified nuns who had a profound influence on children and women. The number of parochial schools increased, and stricter tithing and monetary contributions for baptism, marriage, and death rituals were expected. Priests were encouraged to discourage Mexican-American parishioners against any form of rebellion. Those who did not comply, like Father Antonio Martinez, a Chicano priest in New Mexico, were excommunicated. Non-Spanish-speaking European nuns were brought into the Southwest. In New Mexico, for example, Bishop Jean Baptiste Lamy, an arch-enemy of Father Martinez, brought the sisters of Loretto to Santa Fe in the early 1850s. Their cultural and linguistic influence on the Spanish-speaking women and children lasted until 1968, when the school finally closed. The poor did not attend Catholic schools, however. If they went to school, they went to the public schools. Catholic schools for girls earned income from the tuition paid by the Spanish girls' parents. After the U.S. war with Mexico, Spanish-speaking people had to deal with a new economy based on capital. Not only did Chicanas need to learn to speak English, but now they also needed money.

They also encountered new laws and standards by which their behavior and beauty were measured. White women were considered beautiful. Traditionally, dark complected Catholic women now lived with conflict among whites, who tended to be Protestant but were also Mormons who wanted to convert them. Former Mexicanas saw their religious beliefs, and their customs, degraded and were treated with much rancor.

The socialization of Chicanos into Anglo ways continues until this day, not because Chicanos are slow learners, but because of cultural resistance. Groups integrated into a society via violence are highly resistant to their conqueror's ways. The conqueror does not feel it has to change. Social forces, especially poverty and imprisonment, compel Chicanas to be U.S. citizens, to acclimate themselves to the American eurocentric norm, but in the main they have not because these ways are unacceptable to them.

Resistance can take more subtle forms than violence, such as refusing to speak English or passing one's studies in school in order to have more power (knowledge about Anglos) to resist. The active resistance of former Mexicans to Americanization began before 1848 and the signing of the Treaty of Guadalupe, and continued through the Chicano civil rights movement and the Chicana feminist movement.

After 1848, Mexicanas protested loudly. One of the most verbal among dozens of women was California's Rosalia Vallejo, who refused to interrelate with Anglo Americanos. In one incident, she saved a sixteen-year-old girl from sexual assault by the famed American frontiersman, John Fremont, and his officers. Vallejo was pregnant during the heat of the war and had to be content with writing letters of protest. After the war she referred to Americanos as hated men, who inspired within her large doses of hatred against their race. Even thirty years after her wartime encounters with them, she had not forgotten their insults; she wanted no contact with them and refused to learn their language.

Other California resistance workers included Apolinaria Lorenzana, who suffered the intrusion of an Anglo military officer into her bedroom. She was highly verbal about the indignity and the freedom with which Anglo males penetrated Mexican female space. She loathed speaking of the war even several years later. Another, María Inocente Pico de Avila, was yanked out of school to be trained for marriage to a man who would become the last territorial governor of California. Avila described the male-dominated custom of arranging marriages between thirteen- and fifteen-year-old girls to adult men, especially to American men, with much resentment. Ironically, as mothers it was women who executed the patriarchal agreements. Avila refers to arranged marriages as a "mala costumbre," a bad custom.

Some women, like Eulalia Perez, who has already been mentioned as *la mayordoma*, the supervisor and keeper of the keys at the San Miguel Mission in southern California, led very active lives working outside the home. Perez oversaw most, if not all, the work that took place at the mission. Such grand responsibility was unusual for females at the time. During Perez's time María de las Angustias de la Guerra was a nurse, with strong opinions about the ill effects of the war on Californios, especially the women (Padilla, 1993).

During this period, white American women, like Margaret Fuller, were encouraging women to be more independent. This first round of the white women's movement does not appear to have impacted Mexicanas and Chicanas in any way. Fuller's words and feminist rallies featuring Elizabeth Cady Stanton, Lucy Stone, Harriet Hunt, and the abolitionist

Lucretia Mott did not reach Mexicanas living in the disputed territory. So intense were the disputes that in Mexico, the Mexican War and its outcome are called the North American Invasion or the American Imposition. There was also heavy American resistance to this war in the United States, particularly from David Corwin and Henry David Thoreau. After the war, Chicanas witnessed the debate over which states would be allowed into the union as slave or free states. Some southern states wanted the United States to acquire Cuba and expand the slave territory by taking it from Spain. Chicanas simply wanted the Yankees to go home.

During the aftermath of the war, white ladies of the elite society were wearing dresses of velvet and silk. The basque, a bodice with a short skirt, or tails, under the waistline was a popular fashion (*Chronicle of America*, pp. 340–341). This dress was most unlike that of former Mexicanas living in hot climates who wore full skirts with short-sleeved cotton blouses that mainstream Americanos thought looked more like underclothing. Some of the Mexicanas also went barefoot, but slowly those with money began to dress like American women. Eventually, mestizo women put away the weaving apparatus and purchased clothing from white-owned stores.

DIVIDING THE LAND

After the Gadsden Purchase in 1853—the acquisition of 29,640 square miles of territory for $10 million—Mexicanas saw more and more of their land being fenced off and sold to the railroad, which threatened the indigenous way of life to the point of near extinction. This way of life was even more severely threatened when the Yankees moved into the territory, following the discovery of silver and gold on former Mexican land. White men rushed into the Rocky Mountains past the Great Divide into California, where they were greatly disliked and unwelcome.

Mexicanas were so busy resisting racism and land encroachment that they barely noticed the female activity on the east coast. Nor is there any evidence that an outreach effort was made toward them. In 1859, Susan B. Anthony challenged Anglo men on the issue of slavery. In the South, the African-American Harriet Tubman had helped bring 800 slaves to freedom by 1863. Few Chicanas kept journals, and few Chicanas were written about in the English newspapers of the time. Generally, they were isolated in the Southwest during the time preceding a vicious war; but another U.S. war was taking place, the Civil War, and it did not end until 1865.

In 1864, Maximilian was named the French emperor of Mexico. His rule was imposed by France as a result of Mexico's unpaid debts to France. He was backed by the conservative Junta de Notables and by the large French army. He arrived with his wife, Carlotta, who was known to favor liberal reforms, but from the peasant perspective, her "liberal" ideas were hardly recognizable as such.

Little is known about Chicanas in the Southwest. The KKK was formed in the United States in 1865. Few know of its presence in the Southwest. Even though the organization specifically targeted Chicano males, Chicanas, especially in Texas, came to fear the intrusion of the KKK in their lives. In the mid- to late-1800s many of them saw a black man for the first time when they observed the black cowboys on longhorn cattle drives moving toward the area stockyards. During this period of intense social change the "Americanos" were fighting Indians. Mestizo girls still wore heavy dark stockings and parted their hair down the center of their head, in the traditional Spanish style. Only their faces and forearms were exposed. More change came when women, for the first time in the United States, got the vote in Kansas in 1869. We know nothing about Chicanas in Kansas. There were probably a few Mexicanas in the territory. If early Anglo feminists concerned themselves with them in Kansas Territory, they certainly did not write about it.

To earn money, many Mexicanos got jobs laying track as the railroad expanded. After 1850, Mexicanas witnessed the U.S. wars with Indians and the relocation of indigenous people from ancestral homelands to reservations. Some mestizas even gave indigenous people shelter. As U.S. industrialization expanded, Chicanas nursed their men as they recovered from various industrial accidents and attempted to enter unions.

Some Chicanas went to public school where they observed and experienced the discipline of the ruler, were subjected repeatedly to hair searches for lice, and continually suffered demeaning punishment by Anglo female teachers for speaking their language and for eating their cultural food at lunchtime. Later, during industrialization, Chicanas were forced by law to go to American public schools, where their course work was in English and so they failed. Bronze-colored young women learned how to be neat and ladylike, the American way, and they were taught to speak, read, and write like the Americans. When out of school, they learned to use make-up and to wear American clothing, and eat American food. They saluted the flag, and they celebrated the Fourth of July. A few Mexican-American women even grew up to be teachers, the way American women became teachers. They became instruments of cultural and national oppression without knowing what was happening to them. They did it in the name of education and helping the Mexican American acquire a better way of life. The dominant social-cultural forces behind this effort were so intense and so successful that even today to question the premise is to be un-American.

Racial stereotypes and sexist slurs were common. Chicanas came to hate the words "mamasita" and "greaser." Women's proper names were

Women from all over the world gathered in China to exchange information about the conditions of women in their countries. Photograph by Sandra Romero.

changed, so that Margarita was now Margaret, Maggie, or Marge, and Beatriz was now spelled Beatrice and pronounced differently. Names like Encarnación were translated into meaningless entities. Mexican-American women were made to feel so ashamed of their Mexican names that many changed their names themselves. When they had children, many of them gave their children Anglo names, or the Anglicized version of a Mexican name. Thus, Dorotea became Dorothy, Elena became Helen, and María became Marie or Mary. It was not until the Chicano civil rights movement in the 1960s that these linguistic trends began to be turned around and Chicanas reclaimed their Spanish names.

During the Americanization period that followed the U.S. war with Mexico, Mexican-American women lived two lives: They were Americans in school and other public places, and they were Mexicanas in their homes and segregated communities. They were now further dichotomized so that they had public lives and private lives. Later, in the barrios that sprang up around manufacturing enterprises, many of these women had children who grew up in company towns (Blea, 1990). For many, growing up and enduring Americanization meant engaging in a struggle between what was taught at home and what was taught in school, what was expected and experienced when they were with their own people versus when they were with Anglos. The mothers of these young girls were of a different generation, country, and historical period, and not surprisingly a generation gap was evident in the transition from Mexicana to Chicana.

The Americans brought some interesting innovations, especially the mail order catalog, thread, the sewing machine, cameras, crude washing machines, and tourists. In 1876, they brought news of the telephone, a machine that allowed people to talk over long distances. Long distance was not conceptualized as it is today. In those days it simply meant yards; only later did long distance mean miles. The Americanos also brought the light bulb in 1879. By this time, even poor Chicanos in the rural areas were introduced to the Anglo idea of school and the Anglo woman as school teacher.

Anglo cowboys and rich ranchers became a reality. Few, if any, recognized that Mexicano vaqueros had introduced rodeos and riding the range. In New Mexico, some Nueva Mexicanas (New Mexican women) mourned the death of Billy the Kid, a young unruly "gringo" who liked tortillas and would visit from time to time (Branch, 1980). By this time, the turn of the century, northern and southern Europeans were immigrating by the thousands into the United States and sentiment had turned against Chinese immigration. The Chinese had helped build the railroad, and had provided food, laundry, and other services. But now they were no longer needed, and so Chinese immigration was halted for ten years under the Chinese Exclusion Act of 1882. By the end of the nineteenth century, several other ethnic groups shared the Americanization process. Northern and southern Europeans, like Mexicans, were a cheap source of labor and were frequently played against one another. Because they were white, however, the new immigrants were often hired over Mexicans. A few Mexican women knew that European immigrants were being used against Mexicans in the labor market, and ethnic relations were not always pleasant, but urban Mexicanas came to know the new ethnic people when they went to work in the factories. Later, in the 1930s and 1940s, a few would work together to form strikes and boycotts against the relentless capitalists.

Most Mexicanas were relegated to the home; men didn't want their wives working. Being able to provide for the wife was then considered a measure of male manhood. Some Mexicana houses were larger and better than others, and a class division emerged. At home women had the most power in the areas of childbearing, food preparation, spiritual guidance, and transmission of male-centered cultural information. They adjusted to having men away for many hours during the day but returning dead tired at night. As their land holdings disappeared, the urban Chicano became a reality.

Mexican/Chicano men worked with and for white men; thus, they soon learned English and white ways. The women did not gain this knowledge. Some of the men even went away to places like Wyoming and California to tend and sheer sheep or produce harvest. One area in which la Chicana became stronger was in the holistic practice of medicine in her home. The people could not afford doctors. Young women basically had but two options in life: to become a wife or to become a nun.

The social climate of the period and the reaction to Mexican-American women are highlighted in the writings of Susan Magoffin, one of the few Anglo women in the Texas–New Mexico area during the Anglo conquest (see Cotera, 1976). Magoffin expressed the disgust she felt, viewing Mexican-American women dancing and smoking at their community gatherings. Proper Anglo women were not allowed to do these things.

THE MEXICAN REVOLUTION

While Chicanos were being introduced to the privileges of U.S. citizenship, Mexico continued to develop and impact the lives of its former citizens, who were now U.S. citizens. The Mexican Revolution of 1910 displaced and fragmented families in both Mexico and the United States. Some women responded by becoming activists. Among them were the female soldiers and camp followers known as las Adelitas. Some women also formed la Cruz Blanca, the White Cross, whose role was to nurse soldiers on both sides of the battle over land rights. Jovita Idar organized a large educational and cultural conference in 1911, el Primer Congreso Mexicanista (National Women's History Project, 1992).

Cotera (1976) notes that the Mexican military archives contain the names of thousands of women who were active during the Mexican Revolution. The chaotic situation families lived under prior to and after the war of independence in 1910, and the relatively short period of social and economic stability, did not afford thousands of women much choice than to follow the armies. Women and children were left unprotected from oppositional armies and with few, if any, resources.

Among the heroic figures of the period are Carmen Serdan and Filomena del Valle de Serdan, who organized the first revolutionary forces in Puebla and gathered munitions for the men. For their efforts both were imprisoned by military officials for very long periods. Other women of revolutionary action were Juana Belén Gutiérrez de Mendoza, from Guanajuato, who spent much time in jail for publicizing the revolution in *Vesper* and other publications. Petra Ruiz, Eccha Bala, Encarnación Marés de Panuca, Sra. Carmen Parra Viuda de Alaniz, and Juana Torres became well-known soldiers who acquired the rank of officers. Women also worked behind the lines as clerks and secretaries, smugglers, and telegraphers. Some were even forcibly conscripted into military service. Victoriano Huerta ordered three hundred women from Morelos sent to Quintana Roo in hopes of establishing a colony with men who had been exiled there. The experiment did not work, and the women were returned to Veracruz and abandoned there with the children they bore from their stay in Quintana Roo. To escape the tragedies of war, many Mexican citizens sought asylum in the United States, and many faceless U.S. women of U.S.–Mexican heritage assisted the war effort in Mexico. The women in Mexico strengthened the revolutionary consciousness both in Mexico and the United States by sharing their work on magazines and newspapers (like *La Opinion* in Los Angeles), feminist organizations in Mexico, and by fighting in the battlefields of the Mexican Revolution.

Many of the new immigrants later became U.S. citizens, although they still had family and even businesses in Mexico. Politicians had embroiled Mexico's affairs with the United States, and Mexico owed the United States lots of money. Some would like to believe that Chicana history is consistent with their role in family formation. Although the family is a very important structure, this is not always true. Social and political change have a grand impact on the Chicana's life. The Mexican Revolution is but one example. Another example is the Chicano Movement.

Since the movement, the women who participated in the Mexican Revolution have served as role models for Chicanas. Many Chicanas in the 1960s and 1970s identified with las Adelitas in their attempt to win back their land and identity with the land. Like las Adelitas they also fought for the rights of poor people and opposed racism in urban and rural battlefields. Some Mexican Adelitas rose to high military rank in the Mexican Revolution, and Chicanas questioned why this was not possible in the 1960s. Most of the women of both revolutionary movements cared for family, friends, and neighbors who had been displaced from mainstream society. They cooked and tended the sick, the wounded, and the weary; but the 1960s Chicanas were also writing speeches and giving them to their boyfriends or husbands to deliver, making signs for them to carry, holding fund raisers in order to give the men money to carry on the business of the movement. In their daily activities, las Adelitas suffered the hardships of war, but they were creative and succeeded in keeping many of those involved alive. This caretaker image may be the stereotype, but it reinforced the knowledge of the 1960s Chicano that the general perception of Chicanas as weak, submissive, and unintelligent was not true.

During the Mexican Revolution, the women often traveled with the military to collect the corn that fell from the feed sacks of horses in order to make tortillas. It was also not uncommon for them to use what scarce food sources they had for medicine. Many of them would have their babies, rest for an hour or two, and then catch up with the forces that had moved forward. Many of those women were assisted by other women familiar with the health and healing traditions that had been inherited from their Spanish European and indigenous ancestors. Fifty years later, las Adelitas and the spirit of revolution motivated Chicanas to address conditions of conquest and patriarchy in the Chicano movement.

By 1910, agriculture in the United States had grown into big business. Women, men, and children worked long hours in the sun, where they picked vegetables and weeded the fields. Some women worked in restaurants and laundries, and others in the private homes of white women. Vast numbers of Mexican families came to the United States to escape the battles in Mexico. Approximately one-eighth of Mexico's population immigrated. By 1911, 20,000 U.S. troops were sent to the Mexican border to "protect American interests." The rebellion against Porfirio Díaz, who had ruled Mexico almost continuously since 1876, had now spread so far north that it was affecting the United States directly. Among the Mexican grassroots leaders was Pancho Villa in Chihuahua who was reported to be invading into New Mexico. Emiliano Zapata was leading in the south, and among the "rebels" were las Adelitas, the camp followers and female soldiers whom Americanos viewed as a curiosity or an object of contempt. This revolution delayed the acceptance of U.S. statehood in Arizona and New Mexico. New Mexico became a state only after bitter political resistance to statehood because of U.S. racism, Anglo mining, and land-grabbing tactics. It should be noted that Chicanas who are today only slightly over fifty years old grew up in a union that had only forty-eight states. The memories of resistance to statehood are still living.

REFERENCES

Blea, Irene I. 1990. *La Chicana and the Intersection of Race, Class and Gender*. New York: Praeger.

Branch, Louis Leon. 1980. *Los Bilitos: The Story of Billy the Kid and His Gang*. New York: Carlton Press.

Chronicle of America. 1993. Mount Kisco, N.Y.: Chronicle Publications.

Cotera, Martha. 1976. *Diosa y Hembra*. Austin, Tex.: Information Systems Development.

Enriquez, Evangelina, and Alfredo Mirande. 1979. *La Chicana: The Mexican American Woman*. Chicago: University of Chicago Press.

National Women's History Project. 1992. "Adelante Mujeres." (Video.) Washington, D.C.

Padilla, Genaro M. 1993. *My History, Not Yours: The Formation of Mexican-American Autobiography*. Madison: University of Wisconsin Press.

7

U.S. EXPANSION AND RESISTANCE TO THE AMERICANIZATION PROCESS

During the international women's conference in Mexico City in 1985, I had a chance to meet with some of Mexico's leading female and male feminists. When I asked why men had accompanied the women, they responded that Mexico had a long tradition of feminism and that some men supported civil and human rights for women. They were proud to be feminists because it was the right thing to do. We discussed Chicana feminism, and in conclusion they asserted that Mexican-American women should not give las Adelitas, or the soldaderas, as high a role model position as we had. They maintained that most of the lower class women of the revolution were camp followers reacting to the war decisions of men. They suggested that American women should place more value on the life of Sor Juana Ines de la Cruz, the scholarly feminist nun who questioned the leadership of men, along with their attitudes and behaviors toward women. Perhaps the Mexican feminists were correct, but women should be free to choose their own role models for whatever reasons. Chicanas have adopted women of the Mexican Revolution, as well as Sor Juana Ines de la Cruz, as role models. They see their battle for liberation as involving both theory and practice.

WOMEN OF THE MEXICAN-AMERICAN FRONTIER

The social and political policies during the beginning of the U.S. Americanization period dislocated la Chicana from her former central seat of

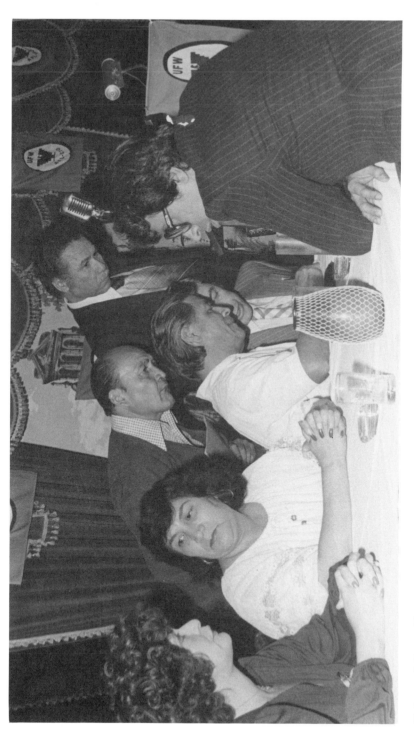

Helen and Cesar Chavez meet with community leaders at a UFW fund-raiser. Photograph by Oscar Castillo.

government and caused her to become alienated from Mexico, as well as from her conqueror. When a new hierarchical political structure favoring whites was inherited, la Chicana's disempowerment was cemented. U.S. popular culture fostered the internalization of a racist social message, so that many Chicanas did not want to be associated with anything as brown as a Mexican. Their goal was to be white, and they could do this by identifying as Spanish European. Chicana stereotypes emerged and are still visible in contemporary sexist and racist popular culture. This is most clearly seen in the jokes based on distorted folklore, misrepresented traditional customs, and the vulgarization of the Spanish language. This perversion increased with the increased migration of white Americans into the Southwest. White cultural values and the English language were put into quick political use, leading to loss of land, which translated into loss of economic and political power.

Early Hispanic society evidenced both racial and class differences. Remnants of these differences are still apparent today. Spanish European-born individuals of the upper class were distinguished by the use of titles. A doña was a high-status female, and a don was a high-status male. Doñas tended to be married or older respected women. A younger woman was a señorita, lady, or little lady. A nonmarried woman was always a señorita. Old records denote other statuses such as married, widowed, or orphaned. In genealogical records, however, nationality and race are frequently recorded, and reference is made to Español (Spanish), criolla (born in the Americas but of Spanish blood), Mexicano (Mexican, or full-blooded mestizo), India (Indian), and mulatta (part Spanish, part African).

Little is known about the interaction of Indian and Hispanic women outside of the worker–employer or doña–servant relationship. By the end of the 1800s, most indigenous peoples of the Southwest had lost much land, and plans were made to relocate them to reservations. Those who resisted (many did) oppression were killed or were tried in English in new U.S. court systems and were found guilty of a few real and many imaginary crimes. Neither a Mexican nor an Indian could win in an English-speaking court, if the case made it to court, especially if they killed white men or were accused of violating white women.

The Spanish-speaking population was engrossed in Americanization struggles and was distanced from the indigenous people by the reservation system and by a new brand of racism that made it unfavorable to identify as "Indians," who had the color red attached to their image. The populations were frequently used against one another. Those who recognized that all indigenous people were also experiencing cultural and physical genocide could do little about it. However, many similarities can be found between the plight of the "Indian" woman and the Mexican woman. All indigenous women were lumped together with no recognition of their diversity. (The same has happened today with U.S. Latinas.) Both were involuntarily incorporated into the United States; both had their people killed in the process; both were subjected to Americanization; both had their language and religion degraded and suppressed; both experienced a change in their economic and social status; both were raped. There were some major differences in how these similarities came to pass, of course. Young Spanish-speaking women were not forcefully taken from their homes and placed in schools as the young Indian females had been. Mexican women were pressured into school out of a need to avoid harassment by officials and in order to learn the colonizer's culture to survive. Mexican women do not have an official body of laws that formally regulate their lives, but there are unwritten laws. Both women had to do what they had to do to survive. This took hard physical, psychological, and spiritual work. Yet, Mexican and "Indian" women were portrayed as fat, lazy squaws—as breeding machines and beasts of burden.

Prior to the U.S. conquest, Indian women had been important figures in their society, responsible for growing produce and hunting small game, which sustained the tribes during and between the hunts. Women, especially mestiza pioneer women, were governed by the needs of their frontier lifestyle. Much like the Haitian and Cuban refugee women of the 1980s and the early 1990s, Indian women were rounded up and detained within the walls of military camps and forts, and prepared for relocation. Although many cultural differences divide them, the racist treatment is still the same. Like the refugee women in Florida, many Indian women got sick and died. When this story is recorded, it is told as if the impact was the same for both sexes, but this is doubtful. Men do not menstruate; they do not give birth; they have greater upper body strength; they are addressed more directly. Nevertheless, many died waiting for the army to decide what to do with them. Some marched with Chief Joseph, and in 1886 the women of Geronimo's resistance wept as the Apache were the last tribe to surrender to whites in Arizona. The Apache did this only after a very difficult and lengthy resistance that covered areas in New Mexico and Arizona. Racist language such as "on the warpath" and racist sayings such as "The only good Indian is a dead Indian" were common and still survive today.

Mexicanas and Indians disappeared from U.S. history. Land grabbing continued, and white America established patterns that would take the United States into its world leadership role. On October 2, 1989, the country hosted the First International Conference of American States, a body consisting of every independent country in the Western Hemisphere, except the Dominican Republic. These countries met to address matters such as arbitration of disputes, adjustment of tariffs, and establishment of a commercial bureau. The official government stand was that the United States sought a Latin American policy of solidarity that could be based on friendship or force. With its political parties well instituted and the wars with the Indians and Mexicans won, the United States settled in, and Chicanas were introduced to Hershey chocolate and Labor Day parades.

It is not recorded whether Chicanas noted the passing of Frederick Douglass, the African-American civil rights leader, in 1885, but African-American civil rights leaders were to become very important to Chicanas in the 1960s. Until then, the Catholic Church played a leading role in their lives. Ten years later the Catholic Pope, Leo XIII, noted the rapid growth of the Catholic Church in the United States. As he praised the freedom of religion in the United States, he failed to mention that the growth of the church was due to the increasing Mexican-American population. Protestants had persecuted American Catholics, especially those of Mexican ancestry. Archbishop Lamy, in New Mexico, excommunicated the Spanish-speaking Penitente, even though this organization had kept the Catholic Church alive during a long absence of priests. The Pope opposed the separation of church and state but did not object to the U.S. political dislocation of the central seat of the Catholic Church from Durango, Mexico to St. Louis, Missouri.

On July 20, 1895, U.S. expansion ambitions demanded that Great Britain submit its dispute with Venezuela over the Guiana boundary, where gold was discovered, to arbitration. The United States had set up the Monroe Doctrine in 1823 as a result of an increasing European threat in Latin America. The doctrine effectively prohibited anyone, other than the United States, from intervening in the Americas. In 1896, the United States then set up a commission on Venezuela and intervened in its dispute with Great Britain by voting to fund it at $1 million. The cumulative effect of these and other efforts was to plant the seeds of the "Third World" in the Western Hemisphere, and set the United States up as the "First World." In 1896, Spain's colonial power was weak, and uprisings had erupted in Cuba. When Spain rejected U.S. arbitration in the conflict, the United States became more sympathetic with the Cuban rebels, thereby increasing U.S. interest and determination to invade Cuba in 1896, when it declared war on Spain over Cuba's fate. In preparation, Theodore Roosevelt's Rough Riders were recruited and trained in San Antonio, Texas, in March. Mexican-American males from San Antonio and as far away as Las Vegas, New Mexico, went to Cuba to fight with the man who would soon be president. Once again, the United States was at war with a Spanish-speaking country over territory. As contemporary feminists have noted, ironically, Spanish-speaking men went to war against Spanish-speaking men in order to prove their "Americanness" to their conqueror. The United States won the war in Cuba, and in 1898, after hearing of the vicious invasion of Santiago, the U.S.

media announced that Puerto Rico had surrendered to the United States. The Spanish-American War resulted in 289 U.S. casualties, but the army lost roughly 4,000 men to diseases like typhoid and yellow fever and to the consumption of chemically tainted beef. Chicano men returned from the war. Chicanas nurtured them and watched them die or waste away in a racist economic system that did not include them. The result of U.S. foreign policy at the turn of the century impacted the lives of current immigrant Latinas in their own country. The United States was deemed superior in all things.

AMERICANIZATION CONTINUES

By the turn of the century, motor cars, trains, and tourists raced across the former Mexican territory, which now had become part of the national park system. The land rush brought many white settlers willing to put up a structure on free land given to them by the government. Most whites came to the Southwest seeking to escape the crowded eastern cities. Even European immigrants were setting up shops in former Mexican territory. We do not know what Chicanas knew about the political times, and we do not know what they knew about the Philippines; but many U.S. whites opposed the annexation of the island as a U.S. territory in 1899.

It is not clear how much Chicanas knew about labor struggles and labor leaders like Mother Jones, but it is reasonable to assume that they had some information because they became involved in the labor movement. Early histories of the women discussed below reveal that they had some knowledge of the issues. During this time, airplanes were flying, and white women were driving automobiles. Chicanas could not afford such luxuries. As white women gained more freedom, the Panama Canal, in yet another Spanish-speaking country, came under construction in 1905. By the time it was completed, white women like Sarah Bernhardt were stars of the American stage. Mexicanas were most unlike these women. In the early 1900s, white and Mexican females alike experienced their most intense interaction in the hierarchical political space of the classroom where white women were the authority, the teacher, and the Mexicana girls and boys the students. By this time, "Americanos" owned farms that were thriving on what the indigenous and the mestizo considered occupied Indian and Mexican land.

There is no evidence that Chicanas noticed the Mann Act, which prohibited the transport of white women across state lines for immoral or sexual purposes. The racial overtones of the act were strong. Mixed relationships were outlawed, and Mexicanas and Indians were accorded the lowest status in the Southwest. Mexicano males were at best laborers after they lost the land and made the difficult transition from rural field to urban factory. This fact gave them experience with white men. The women were isolated in their homes.

Until the 1990s, each generation of Mexicanas saw their men march off to war. Contemporary Chicanas had great-great grandfathers who fought in World War I. In the 1940s after World War II, their fathers came home as some of that war's most highly decorated men. Their brothers fought and died in Korea, the first war that was never declared a war; and they died disproportionately in Vietnam. Chicanas received their husbands and sons in body bags, or they watched helplessly as they were either destroyed by the effects of Agent Orange, drug addiction, and alcoholism, or committed suicide. Many women reared children alone because Chicano men could not readjust and landed up in prison. All of these tragic effects are not counted in the war casualty statistics, and it is not unusual then that for the first time in history Mexican-American culture has experienced so many women living without male partners. Now their daughters await the side-effects of the Gulf War.

It took years to learn about the American female experience in Vietnam, and the Vietnamese woman still has to write her story. Were it not for Margarethe Cammermeyer, a military colonel and gay activist, it might have taken a similar length of time to discover that women serving in Vietnam, especially nurses, were constantly threatened with rape (Cammermeyer and Fisher, 1994). Cammermeyer reports that guards were stationed at their tents to protect them from U.S. servicemen who might rape them. She faced continual harassment and discrimination because of her gender and sexual orientation. Neither the Chicana experience in Vietnam nor the African-American female experience has been documented. In the early 1990s, the same Chicanas saw their sons and grandsons go to the Gulf War to fight people who looked like their sons and grandsons. All the while, Chicanos and Chicanas were being discriminated against in jobs, education, the health arena, and the criminal justice system. It should be noted that both Chicanos and Native Americans are American citizens, with formal rights and privileges. They are the populations who have treaties with the United States which have been systematically violated.

Men make war and women endure this patriarchal phenomenon that causes such profound historical trauma. Even today, those seeking to Americanize Chicanas may not see their actions as harmful, but they were indeed destructive. Techniques that were considered good industrial sociology and psychology transferred a social work mentality from the workplace to the schools. The earliest contention was that ethnic children would grow up to be good workers. In a study of Bessemer (Blea, 1990), the daughters and wives of steel mill workers were introduced to the latest labor-saving appliances, with the intent of manipulating them into pressuring male workers at the mill into working harder to earn money in order to purchase the latest appliances. Colorado Fuel & Iron officials never encouraged ethnic males and females to leave the mill to seek higher education, to become doctors, lawyers, corporation owners, and other professionals. Instead, it cemented into the minds of the early Bessemer population the roles of working-class men and women by teaching them a common language, English, homemaking, American hygiene, and manners.

Americanization took place through the missionary work of white women among Mexican women and children. Contemporary Chicanas know that the United States selects, borrows, or simply integrates aspects of Chicano culture that are convenient for producing profit. They see little respect for their language or their skin color in advertising these products. Thus, it is widely believed that the dominant U.S. population is concerned with Chicanos only to the degree that they can maximize profit. Much effort has gone into centralizing whiteness and the Protestant ethic.

One of the most pervasive myths about the United States is that all the country's people immigrated and wanted to be U.S. citizens. Keep in mind that the Chicanos are conquered people and that Latinos have unknowingly inherited this legacy. New Mexico and Arizona resisted statehood the longest; but the Chicanos resisted statehood in Texas, California, and Colorado. After having conquered the territory, elections were held to decide whether the territories wanted statehood. With more whites politically active in their own structure, in their own interest Chicano resistance manifested itself in losing the vote over statehood. Conquered people do not conform easily, and political resistance is evident even today. White–Chicano differences are more visible during every election, but conflict is evidenced everywhere. Of extreme interest here is that most Latinas still refer to white women as "Americanas," just as they did before the U.S. war with Mexico.

In the early 1900s, racism and sexism were well entrenched, but class issues were at the forefront of national attention with the U.S. labor movement, and Lola Chavez de Armijo addressed sexism in her personal campaign involving job-related discrimination, politics, and court battles. Her agitation efforts resulted in the first documented case of job discrimination based on gender in the early months of New Mexico's statehood (Díaz, 1992). Armijo was the state librarian in New Mexico. Governor William C. McDonald began a campaign to oust her from her position by spreading the notion that women were not qualified to hold appointive political office. McDonald lost his case and appealed to the Supreme Court, which ruled against him.

In the early 1900s, U.S. troops were deposing Victoriano Huerta in

Mexico while Chicanas and Chicanos were being massacred during a strike at the Ludlow mine in Colorado. This bloody massacre of eighteen people—three men, two women, and thirteen children—took place in 1914, the year Mother's Day was declared a national holiday. White women were also resisting establishment mores. Margaret Sanger was fleeing from authorities, who wanted to arrest her for writing and distributing a newspaper that maintained such ideas as a woman had a right to control her own body. She was not indicted, until she tried to distribute a pamphlet outlining the use of birth control with sponges, diaphragms, and other devices. She could have been sentenced to forty-five years in prison. We have no information on how U.S. Mexicanas reacted to Sanger, or even if they knew about the controversy. What we do know is that these women tended to have as many children as "God" gave them, and that today a woman's right to control her own body is an issue all over the world.

U.S. involvement in Mexico impacted the Mexicanas gravely because so many Mexicans left Mexico to come to live in the United States in order to escape the war. Some of today's Chicana feminists are descendants of people who lived through the Mexican Revolution. During and after the revolution, Mexicanas traveled north, often alone, and settled in places like El Paso, San Antonio, and various barrios in Los Angeles. Many of them were single women who had family in the United States or who appeared at the doors of Catholic churches seeking work and other forms of assistance. Many of these women encountered missionaries who generally sought converts away from the Catholic faith. The women also had many novel experiences. For instance, they were introduced to "American" health care and were lucky if it was delivered in a bilingual environment. Their goal was generally to become homemakers, but some had experiences with scouting, piano lessons, dance, and bible school. All were introduced to English, and some went to school, where they learned civics and literature. Most were also part of the unwritten americanization program aimed at getting immigrant women to conform to the American way of life from approximately 1910 to the end of World War II.

Catholic priests became part of the Americanization process. Many were racist and they scared Chicanos. The idea of sin was a common deterrent for many things not Catholic. During this time, the priests told parishioners that it was a sin to go to a Protestant church or to interact with Protestants. The priests wanted more money from poor *raza* and often complained about pennies in the collection baskets. The most vicious of these controlling campaigns was waged against the Indian schools. Most of the priests held patronizing attitudes toward the indigenous and as a result indigenous children ran away. Meanwhile, Mexicanas tried to teach their children human decency. They told their children they were to resist contact with white people, but if contact were made, they were to be polite.

Some Mexican women were recruited as liaisons between the missionaries and the Mexican community. These women were not trusted by the Spanish-speaking community and so were often ostracized. Chicanas refused to embrace the romantic idea of americanization because of the contrast between the ideal and the real. The picture painted of life in the United States by the schools, the teachers, and the missionaries was in stark contrast to their experiences with the ramifications of racism.

Heavy European immigration continued, and a play entitled *The Melting Pot* gave substance to an assimilation theory that many still embrace today. Basically, the premise is that the United States is a big pot where ethnics blend together to become a homogeneous country. There is no explanation as to where the heat, the element that forces the melting, comes from. Social pressure emanates from the integrated, intersecting, americanization forces that are so clearly evident in education, politics, economics, religion, the health system, and the criminal justice network. Color plays a key role here. White ethnics assimilated quite well, but people of color were discriminated against in U.S. institutions.

When World War I began in Europe and U.S. mobilization was proposed, white women protested, saying, "I didn't raise my boy to be a soldier." This female sentiment has not disappeared. The year before the war, in 1916, U.S. troops were still involved in Mexico, looking for Pancho Villa, the hero of the Mexican Revolution, claiming he had attacked U.S. citizens. Women had resisted U.S. involvement in the revolution, but 18 American soldiers were killed by Mexican forces on June 21, 1916, when the United States entered Mexico.

During this period, the U.S. Senate ratified a treaty under which Nicaragua authorized the United States to build a canal across Central America and a naval base on the Gulf of Fonseca. Honduras, Costa Rica, and El Salvador adamantly opposed the plan, but the United States mobilized its major interests in these countries and was able to silence the protest. The United States' push–pull economic and political relationship with Central and South American countries is seen as rooted in an insatiable need for territory, profit, and military control, and is bitterly resented by citizens of those countries.

Because Chicanas were geographically and socially removed from international policy and white feminist action we do not know their reactions to the National American Woman's party meeting at which President Woodrow Wilson was pushed to support woman's suffrage and an amendment to the U.S. Constitution granting women the right to vote. In reaction to the critical activism of women, and the criticism arising over the direction in which white men in power were taking the country, in late 1916, Catholics were warned that "alien radicalism" in the form of socialism could corrupt American youth, and that the Church would not tolerate divorce. The next year World War I began, and soon thereafter the violent Russian Revolution had the U.S. uneasy over Russia's role in the war. The Russian Revolution resulted in a redistribution of land and spread talk of communism, especially in the United States. "Red baiting," a practice by which activists were accused of being outside communist agitators (as occurred during the Chicano civil rights movement), had its origin in this monumental event.

Mexico had just undergone a similar revolution with similar results just south of the U.S. border, and the threat of alternative government models loomed large in the minds of international policymakers. When Chicanas began their own self-study of Mexican history, they learned that their public education had omitted major world events like the Mexican and the Russian revolutions. Their political displacement, coupled with the omission of their history from public education, awakened in them a need to publicly address the stark dissimilarities between the ideals, the manifest purpose of education, and the real function of americanization. They interpreted the exclusions not only as a form of americanization, but also as a purposeful politicalization of the masses. However, red baiting took place, and few other Mexican-American women wanted much to do with "radical" Chicanas.

A preview of U.S. history and the U.S. experience of Latinas must focus on April 1918, when an estimated 1.4 million women propelled the wartime workforce as they replaced men who were fighting World War I in Europe. They not only had jobs as assembly-line workers, but they were also welders welding bomb casings, delivering coal, and steeple jacking. Very few Latinas were secretaries, and mostly white women served as yeomen in the navy, but some served the United States at the same time that they ran their households while the men were away at war. In 1918, the Spanish flu affected one-quarter of the nation, resulting in the devaluation of Spanish-speaking Americans in the minds of at least one out of every four persons in the United States who suffered with influenza. At the same time, women where working both inside and outside of the home, tending the ill and burying the loved ones who did not survive the Spanish flu. It is harmful to the social health of the nation when devaluation of people of color is often consistent with epidemics that the U.S. health system cannot control. For example, when Asians are targeted, the flu is called the Asian flu. This social tendency to victimize the latest scapegoat population was most recently seen when AIDS was linked to Africa as the place of origin. When this origin could not be validated, gay men were targeted. When lesbian women demonstrated only a low level of AIDS, few medical practitioners pointed out this fact.

The communist idea that the riches of a country should be shared equally among all people spread throughout the globe, increasing the fear of many white capitalists in control in the United States. As a result, more intensified efforts were launched to control these ideas. Those critical of conditions in the United States continued to be "red baited," a labeling that acted to deter the public from listening to critical voices. The label became so powerful that the public was intimidated and saw any critical voice as a threat to the American way of life. They also became vigilant of their own behavior; fearful that they might be labeled communist, they were silenced.

When Chicanas resolved to speak against the conditions of their people and of themselves as women, they were forced to reeducate themselves in their spare time. The fundamental contradiction of the rights guaranteed by the Constitution of justice for all and freedom of speech soon became very clear. White American repression of critical voices was intense throughout the Chicano movement, but it was also evident in Central and Latin American countries.

In 1920, just over seventy years after the Chicanos were conquered by the United States, women were finally guaranteed the vote. American women were successful in ratifying the Nineteenth Amendment during the era of the flapper, Isadora Duncan, and the first of many white Miss America pageants. For Chicanas, all this was secondary to the fact that in 1921 the United States experienced a sharp economic decline and a depression set in, causing heavy white resistance to Mexican workers. The situation intensified to the extent that several hundred Americans of Mexican descent were deported to Mexico. Some of the deportees were deported as families (Balderama and Rodriguez, 1994). Mexican immigration was halted, racism increased ferociously, and stereotypes that still haunt *raza* today emerged. Mexicans and Mexican Americans were described as being reduced to the fundamental functions of beasts: eating, sleeping, and procreating. The population was described as filthy, with insatiable appetites for sex, which resulted in miserable children ridden with disease and lice. Their homes were seen as shacks infested with bed bugs and flies. The women were characterized as slovenly and lazy, subsisting on beans and unable to do anything about their husbands' drunkenness and infidelity. These "dirty women" lounged around all day, totally irresponsible with their bastard children, and apathetic about life. It was among these stereotypes that the mothers and grandmothers of today's Chicanas grew up. The stereotypes became embedded in both the white and Chicano psyche. Anglo-identified whites were held up as superior, and Chicanos, especially Chicanas who had no work or profit-related value, became inferior.

CHICANAS AND THE NEW DEAL

In 1924, immigration quotas based on ethnicity were set almost at half what they had been in 1921. Immigration from Mexico was still allowed, but little was apportioned to other Latin American countries. While Mae West was popular and flaunting her sexuality, and Georgia O'Keeffe was living in New Mexico painting her sensual blossoms, by the end of the "Roaring Twenties" the stock market had crashed. The cartoon character, Blondie, was introduced as a bird-brained housewife serving an even more mentally debilitated husband named Dagwood. Cities grew even more crowded, and unemployment rose sharply. Franklin D. Roosevelt was elected president of the United States in 1932, promising a "New Deal" for the U.S. working person. Progress was the national objective.

Chicanas and Chicanos, complaining about working conditions, retreated inside their *mutualistas* (self-help societies) and aligned with forces moving toward unionization. In 1935, the Works Progress Administration (WPA) was established and employed roughly one-third of the nation's 11 million jobless men. Some white women gained some advantage, but mostly young men, including Chicanos, worked on government projects. There is no record of Chicana involvement, but some were beginning to unionize. Chicano males participated in the Civilian Conservation Corps (CCC) projects that "improved" the national parks, especially in New Mexico, Arizona, and Colorado, while the women stayed home. In 1935, Dorothea Lange's photos of poor white Americans became famous. Some WPA workers photographed Chicana poverty. This era witnessed many labor strikes, conflicts among unions about allowing workers of color to become members, and finally the formulation of the American Federation of Labor (AFL). There was a division of this craft union, which resulted in the Congress of Industrial Organizations (CIO). Eventually, the two merged to form the powerful AFL-CIO, of which my own father and the fathers of many other Chicanas were members.

Unions were red baited, rumored to be infested with communism, and violence became common. It is in this context that Lucy Gonzales Parsons, Emma Tenayuca, and Luisa Moreno rose to national prominence in the bloody American labor movement. During this movement, following World War II, contemporary Chicano class consciousness was solidified, and race/ethnic consciousness began to form. Men were the primary beneficiaries of this movement, but the experience moved the Chicano agenda from regional to national forms of resistance. By the late 1960s, class and race/ethnic consciousness was firm among large numbers of both females and males. It crossed generational lines and became a concentrated effort to change the quality of life for *raza*, but women had special needs that men could not foresee or value. Changing the quality of life for *raza* meant redefining history and social movements, so that they would include Chicanas and Chicanos. It also meant redefining social institutions and decentralizing whiteness.

During the 1930s, some Chicanas and Chicanos joined the Communist party. When Chicanas were able to advance the contributions of women, Emma Tenayuca's participation in the San Antonio, Texas, pecan shelling strike in 1938 was finally documented. Chicano males were quick to publicize her story. Tenayuca was the principal organizer and spokesperson of the strike, representing primarily Chicana workers. Workers were protesting low wages and unsanitary, unsafe work conditions. Women were not even allowed to go to the bathroom. They shelled cans of pecans by hand and were only paid for deshelled quantities of nuts. The strike was extremely successful, but lost its significance when the processing plants were mechanized and machines displaced the workers. Worker displacement remains a labor issue, and Tenayuca engaged in dialogue over such issues until the late 1980s. I had the pleasure of knowing Emma, who at the time of this writing was in a nursing home struggling with Alzheimer's disease. Amazingly, she did not realize her contribution to the class struggle until scholars began to talk to her. She was a critical thinker who made the Chicanos aware of the intellectual component of their civil rights movement. It was based in an ideology that noted the interaction between class, race, and ethnicity.

During the time of Tenayuca's organizing, mostly white artists and writers were supported economically by WPA. The WPA made available $300 million to support the collection of oral histories, to conduct research, and to produce guidebooks. Chicanos, much less Chicanas, were not included in this artist-support effort in any real numbers, but Anglo women and men painted murals in post offices, on school walls, and other public buildings. It was during this time that Chicanos, then known as Spanish Americans or Mexican Americans, became research objects for Anglos, who turned their attention to the less political aspects of Chicano culture: religion, agricultural techniques, stories about their ancestors, and settlement patterns. Nevertheless, they helped document the existence of raza and their poverty.

Meanwhile, as fascism was on the rise in Europe, the curly haired child actress, Shirley Temple, whistled, danced, and said cute, or heart-wrenching, things at the movies and Eleanor Roosevelt was frequently in the media. The depression continued, as did demonstrations and other protests, escalating into violence between protestors and the keepers of the status quo. It is in this context that Luisa Moreno and Josefina Fierro emerged. They, together with many faceless and nameless Chicanas, worked to secure job safety and security, healthy working conditions, equal pay, and benefits for Chicano workers.

In 1935, the Social Security Act was passed providing pensions for Americans over the age of 65, but it did not go into effect until 1942 (*Chronicle of America*, 1993) because of political resistance. Contemporary senior Chicanas who are citizens, as many Americans, depend on Social Security in their senior years (Torres-Gill, 1992).

Perhaps it was when the Roosevelt administration declared the South an economic problem, with conditions so severe that it placed the United States at risk, that contemporary race relations moved into the national spotlight as a black–white issue excluding other groups. This was the case until Michael Harrington wrote *The Other American* in 1963. It had been a black–white issue too long. Mexican Americans and Native Americans were just as poor as the blacks, just as discriminated against, and with the exception of actually becoming slaves, just as oppressed.

In the 1930s, the United States recognized the dictator, Francisco Franco, in Spain. Hispanos (the Spanish word for Hispanics), Chicanos, and Mexicanos may have severed political ties with Spain, but emotional links remained. After all, they spoke the same language, and it was the home of their European ancestors, providing some refuge from intense discrimination. Thus, many Chicanos claimed to be Spanish. This was as close to being white as they could get. There is no known record of how the Spanish-speaking citizens of the United States felt about Franco and his ruthless regime in Spain, but emotional ties to Spain remain strong even today. This was frequently a topic of conversation in the mid-1970s, when I began a long relationship with a refugee professor from Spain, Dr. Domingo Ricart. Ricart had fled Spain with his young wife, other members of the Quaker religion, and one hundred children, walking over the Pyrenees into France in order to ensure the future of a liberated Spain in the next generation. Perhaps, like Ricart's actions on behalf of the next generation of Spaniards, and like the actions of the Jews who claimed to be Catholic during the Inquisition, Chicanos passing as Europeans insured the Chicano's survival to the next generation.

Until they go to college, Chicanitas, young Chicanas, do not learn about those who have struggled to keep their voices alive. They grow up centralized in whiteness and patriarchy. Like their mothers and grandmothers who were affected by white movies such as *Gone with the Wind* and *The Wizard of Oz*, Chicanas were affected by these messages about deviating from traditional U.S. roles for women and the consequences of leaving home. Ideas of the homeland as nurturing and as the only place to be were firmly instilled. The Chicana's centralization of whiteness and heterosexuality became entrenched when television crept into the barrios, and the people watched programs produced by white,

European-centered men, about the glory of manhood in women's lives in the all-American-home.

Earlier, however, by 1941, powerful white U.S. males decided that the country would enter the war in Europe. Chicano and other men went to fight it. World War II, just like World War I, caused a severe shortage of workers. Female entry into the job market was delayed by the Emergency Labor Program of 1942, which brought the first Mexican braceros into the United States in 1943. Mexican "guest workers" who left their women at home were allowed into the United States to work. Some of those men married U.S.-born Chicanas, but not without difficulty because much anti-Mexican sentiment pervaded. Some of the men were already married, and had Chicana girlfriends in the United States. Some were rumored to have married in order to become citizens and of course, many women were used. Mexican men were stereotyped as *mujereros*, womanizers seeking sex and permanent residency. The parents of U.S.-born Chicanas did not want their daughters marrying men of lower status, for they were low enough as Chicanos. Most of the Mexican men sent money home to provide for family. Eventually, Mexican women immigrated with very little money or knowledge about the United States. Women of that era recount the hardship of having to decide to leave their children in Mexico while they made their way north to reunite with their husbands or get work in the United States. For the most part this immigration was legal. Women simply paid their few cents at the border and came into the country. Later, they got work in laundries, meat markets, hotels, and clothing factories. Some of those women are now senior citizens and find memories of this part of their lives so painful that they refuse to talk about it.

Mrs. Gomez (the name has been changed) of Los Angeles, California, was one of those women who stayed behind during the Bracero Program. She has one daughter who still will not talk to her because of anger over having been left in Mexico while Mrs. Gomez worked in the United States at a series of menial jobs. Mrs. Gomez simply could not earn enough money to send for her children. "I didn't abandon them," she pleaded to me in Spanish. "I came out of necessity." The men worked on farms and railroads, and took hazardous jobs like mining. In Mexico there was a great deal of worker organizing, and the men brought this knowledge with them. The formulation of el Partido Liberal Mexican (PLM) impacted both U.S. Mexicans and Mexican Americans. The PLM included women and children employed in textile mills. The newspaper, *Regeneration*, carried countless articles about the participation of women in PLM organizing.

WORKING CHICANAS

Women who worked outside of the home during World War II were commemorated in the song "Rosie the Riveter," but some even joined the military. Chicanas did not join the military at the same rate as white women, but they participated in the war effort by working in shipyards, on trains, and in the ammunition factories. U.S. Chicanas have an extensive history in the labor movement. Lucy Eldine Gonzales, a national labor figure from Johnson County, Texas, married Albert Parsons, who was a self-proclaimed anarchist. With her husband, Gonzales published newspapers, pamphlets, and books, traveled and lectured extensively, and led demonstrations. In the 1870s, she was a charter member of the Chicago Working Women's Union, and in 1905, she was a founding member of the Industrial Workers of the World (IWW). Twenty-two years later she was elected to the National Committee of the International Labor Defense. Gonzales, like the women who came before her, had insight into the intersection of race, class, and gender. She believed that the abolition of capitalism would produce racial and sexual equality. Gonzalez's involvement went beyond national to international issues; she did not focus organizing efforts solely on Mexican workers (Acuna, 1988). One of the major issues for organizers at that time was the dual wage system. Workers, including Mexicans, received lower wages than Anglos doing the same job. This was true even among the women. Mexican women were in the lowest paid and most vulnerable jobs. Even in the laundries Anglo women were in the skilled jobs and Mexicanas in the unskilled. Mexicanas earned half as much as Anglo women. This also was true in department stores, where Anglo women generally worked on the main floor, and Mexicanas worked in the rear or in other less visible parts of the building where lower status and lower paying tasks were performed. Even when visible, Anglos were supervisors; Mexicanas were the clerks. In the garment industry in Texas, the low wages and overrepresentation of Mexicana workers were defended by employers, who claimed that Anglo women outworked Mexicanas, and that an insufficient number of white women were willing to work. The general standard of living among Mexicanas was much lower than the whites' (Acuna, 1988).

In the 1930s the Spanish painter Pablo Picasso painted Gertrude Stein, the white lesbian writer and patron of the arts, who had lived in Paris since 1903. Few U.S. citizens have ever understood Picasso's contribution to the art world via cubism. They better understood Mother Cabrini, Francis Xavier Cabrini, who became the first American saint during this period. Few, however, know Chicana activist Francisca Reyes Esparza, who had a leading role in land rights struggles over raza displacement from their land. While attempting to gather evidence to file a land grant lawsuit for titles to a quarter of a million acres of oil and ranch land, Esparza successfully developed communication between the United States and Mexico. She became an expert on the historical aspects of old land titles guaranteed to Mexican-American citizens under Article VIII of the Treaty of Guadalupe Hidalgo. In 1946, she won her land rights case and set in motion vehicles that are utilized today in similar cases. Esparza's postwar contributions were overshadowed by those of Burt Corona, who is still praised by today's Chicano leaders and academics for the labor causes he so rightfully pursued.

Another Chicana overshadowed by male attention to Corona is Josefina Fierro who became active during the mass deportations (repatriation) of both undocumented Mexicans and Chicano U.S. citizens in the 1930s. Fierro was active in returning Mexican-American citizens, who had wrongly been deported, to the United States from Mexico. In the early 1940s, she joined Corona in organizing low-paid Chicano workers employed in canneries and on farms. Fierro later was also instrumental in ending the violent racist and sexist conflicts between Chicano citizens and U.S. servicemen during World War II in Los Angeles. By negotiating with Vice President Wallace to declare Los Angeles out of bounds to military personnel, Fierro became the most important figure in ending what became known as the Zoot Suit riots.

Chicanas entered the workforce in much larger numbers during the mid-1940s. During World War II, when Hitler sought to control the world via white dominance, not many Chicanas joined the Women's Army Auxiliary Corps (WAAC), nor were they accepted into the Volunteer Emergency Services, the WAVES. Unlike some Anglo women, they did not fly planes, but they did help build them. They filled the nation's arsenals with war instruments and guns. They participated in the war effort in other ways: by collecting tin cans and using stamps to purchase olive oil instead of lard because there was a shortage of lard with which to make tortillas. They waited for the men to return shell shocked, maimed, or dead, and they went on raising children and maintaining their households. They and their children were not counted as part of the war effort or the casualties of war, when their standard of living decreased due to the lack of an adult male income.

During this time, Roosevelt died and was succeeded in the presidency by Harry Truman. Huge media campaigns had fashioned opinion to the point where U.S. citizens learned to fear and hate the Japanese. U.S. Japanese citizens were placed in U.S. detention camps, but U.S. Germans were left alone. The Germans may well have escaped detention because they were white and unlike the Japanese, who often were referred to as the yellow peril, they did not attack the U.S. colony of Hawaii. Color was prominent in Chicana minds as they worked in the shipyards and rail yards until the men returned from military service. During this time, the Zoot Suit riots took place; these disturbances were both racist and sexist in nature. Chicanas were slandered by U.S. servicemen and news media as cheap prostitutes, infected with venereal disease and addicted to marijuana. This slander led to the harassment of Chicanas, and Chicanos wearing zoot suits were often beat up. Interviews with ex-Zoot Suit defendants revealed that Chicanos felt that Chicanas were "their women" and did not want to share them with the "gringo" who often felt the women were readily available for sex. Much fighting took place, and today Chicanas still suffer from these racist/sexist stereotypes.

The end of the war physically reunited men and women, bringing about the baby boom; these baby boomers are now over fifty years of age. Some Mexican-American men took advantage of the G.I. Bill, which offered benefits to those who had served in the military, and went to college. A good number of these higher educated men met and married white women. In spite of their military service, some of these men could not gain admittance to the Veterans of Foreign Wars male clubs set up to celebrate wartime action. After the war, Chicanas stayed home, especially after having lost their jobs to the returning males. A mass media campaign now marketed labor-saving devices directly to women. Much money was to be made in reestablishing women in the home. Home cleaning products were even sold, door to door, by men to women. Largely because of the G.I. Bill, which provided housing benefits, the suburbs were growing, and many whites moved into track housing. New home appliances now allowed white women to do more work, with better quality, isolated in their new houses away from former neighborhoods and people of color.

In 1946 Benjamin Spock wrote *Spock's Common Sense Book of Baby and Child Care* (Weitz, 1977). This book taught white women how to be the best mothers possible by obsessing them about what to expect from their children as they developed. Soon women were consumed with rearing children, and within two years Rosie and Rosita the Riveter had been effectively removed from the line of material production to human production and relegated to roles of superconsumer. Chicanas inherited this mind-set as more of them moved to the cities, where there were jobs for men.

In the 1950s, the nation was afflicted with McCarthyism. The United States' we–they campaign against communism produced terror in many quarters, especially Hollywood, academia, and labor. The first generation of contemporary Chicana feminists grew up during this time, a time when Mexican-American female activity consisted of raising children and going to church. Schoolchildren ducked and cowered under school desks during the "cold war" exercises, in case of nuclear attack. There were no gunshots fired, but words were consistently fired at the young psyche. Men, women, and children all sought protection from the red

Russians, who lived behind the iron curtain and wanted to kill U.S. citizens with their powerful bombs.

Chicanas did not share in the whites' increased standard of living in the late 1940s and 1950s. In fact, they were among the nation's poorest members. To address this inequity the League of United Latina American Citizens (LULAC) and the GI Forum were established; these organizations were designed to ensure the rights of Mexican Americans, and women were very much involved. The emergence of these organizations sparked political activity around the issue of race and ethnicity.

REFERENCES

Acuna, Rodolfo. 1988. *Occupied America: A History of Chicanos*. 3rd ed. New York: Harper and Row.

Balderama, Francisco E., and Raymond Rodriguez. 1994. *Decade of Betrayal: Mexican Repatriation in the 1930s*. Albuquerque: University of New Mexico Press.

Blea, Irene I. 1991. *Bessemer: A Sociological Perspective of a Chicano Barrio*. New York: AMS Press.

Cammermeyer, Margarethe, and Chris Fisher. 1994. *Serving in Silence*. New York: Viking. New York: Recorded Books, Inc.

Chronicle of America. 1993. Mount Kisco, N.Y.: Chronicle Publications.

Dale, Bruce, and Joel Sartore. 1996, February. "Tex Mex Border." *National Geographic*, pp. 44–69.

Diaz, Rose. 1992. "Lola Chavez de Armijo, 1858–1929." In ed., Tey Diana Rebolledo, *Nuestra Mujeres*. Albuquerque: University of New Mexico Press.

Harrington, Michael. 1963. *The Other American: Poverty in the United States*. Baltimore, Md.: Penguin.

Torres-Gill, Fernando M. 1992. *The New Aging: Politics and Change in America*. Westport, Conn.: Auburn House.

Weitz, Shirley. 1977. *Sex Roles: Biological, Psychological, and Social Function*. New York: Oxford University Press.

8

CHICANA FEMINIST MOVEMENT

The United Nations' Fourth World Women's Conference and the Conference that preceded it placed feminism within a global context. Prior to these meetings, women had struggled for women's rights in the isolation of their own countries. In China, a meeting of an estimated 36,000 women, together with media efforts, brought international attention to the fact that women's human rights needed to be defined and protected around the world. In the United States, just a few months after the women's conference, Leticia Sotero Vasquez brought the plight of Latinas from underdeveloped countries to international media attention. She and several others had left their countries of origin through a hazardous journey into Mexico in order to enter the United States in search of work. Sotero Vasquez and her traveling companions simply wanted to better their extraordinarily low standard of living that was the result of the push–pull economic and political relationship between the United States and Mexico. At the Mexico–California border, the pickup truck housing the seventeen passengers in a camper shell ran the crossing at a high speed. California sheriff's officers, suspecting that the passengers might be illegal aliens, pursued the truck on a lengthy chase covering many miles of freeway. Terrified of capture, the passengers began to dismantle the shell of their pickup in order to stall the sheriff's patrol cars long enough for the truck to stop and the passengers to run. They failed in their efforts. When the truck stopped, some of the passengers ran off,

Irene I. Blea speaking at the NGO Conference in Huairou. Photograph by Sandra Romero.

but Riverside sheriff's officers attacked the truck ferociously, beating the passengers, including Leticia Sotero Vasquez.

This incident sparked tremendous national controversy and shocked the white citizens of the nation, but people of color were not surprised. They know that undocumented workers and citizens of color are consistently brutalized by the police and military. They do not trust these officials and are even terrorized by the presence of the police. This mistrust and fear is rooted in the racism and function of white supremacy and the police, which represents this mentality, in the United States. For this reason U.S. women of color established a coalition urging the U.N. Platform on women's rights to include a statement that would feminize racism. Just as poverty became a feminist issue, so women of color were successful in getting into the international document in 1995 the idea that most women in the world are women of color and that most of them endure racism (through war and economic and political exploitation) at the hands of white supremacists. It took thirty years to accomplish this goal.

CHICANO STUDIES

For thirty years Chicanas have demanded that the civil and human rights of Latinos be recognized and protected by the United States. This demand is defined and guaranteed by the Treaty of Guadalupe Hidalgo (1848), the document that made northern Mexico the U.S. Southwest at the end of the U.S. war with Mexico. Richard Griswold del Castillo, a Chicano academic, has provided an historical overview of how various Chicano organizations have interpreted and attempted to utilize the Treaty of Guadalupe Hidalgo to establish a tradition of analysis and strategy for political action in order to ensure human rights for the Chicano community (Garcia et al., 1988). Chicano academics are frequently criticized as being political and not academic.

In the 1970s, young Chicano Studies scholars became very critical of white academic perspectives of the Chicano community. They also presented their own insider perspective as opposed to the outsider perspective in order to provide a less biased picture. They publicly extended the Treaty of Guadelupe Hidalgo and emphasized that the educational, economic, and political system did not reflect their representation and experience. Chicanas began to conduct their own studies on their own communities, but they discovered analytical weaknesses in both white studies and Chicano (male) studies of the community, its history, economy, and politics. This criticism motivated a move from class and race to gender analysis. They moved past criticizing the work by Ruth Tuck, *Not with the Fist* (1946), as severely culturally biased, and they incorporated the first published criticisms by Octavio Romano in "The Anthropology and Sociology of the Mexican Americans" (1968). They stopped citing the Anglo scholarship of Florence Kluckhohn (1961), Celia Heller (1966), William Madsen (1964), Richard Lamanna and Julian Samora (1967), and did their own community studies. The work of Deluvina Hernández, *Mexican American Challenge to a Sacred Cow* (1970), motivated my own research on Bessemer, a Chicano barrio in southern Colorado. Hernández was among the first contemporary Chicanas to be published. Some Chicanas entered the Marxist dialogue and were red baited. The anticommunist movement, which was at its height in the 1950s, when these women were roughly eight to ten years of age, had impressed upon them memories of hiding under crude school desks, fearing the communists would attack while they were away from their families. For this highly visual Chicanita, the "iron curtain" was an enormous, heavy, steel curtain blocking out the Russians, keeping them separated from Americans for security reasons.

In the 1950s, these Chicana scholars were surrounded by labor-saving appliances they could not afford. On television they saw well-dressed white women cleaning gleaming floors in new houses with new mops and floor wax. When the United States backed South Korea against North Korea, most Chicanas did not understand the struggle. They were less confused when they buried brothers and sons in a war that was declared a "police action." In the 1950s, most Chicanas did not understand what the Chinese had to do with Korea; nor did they know who the critical "communist" Rosenbergs were. When the Rosenbergs were convicted for selling U.S. secrets, they did understand that to be critical meant you were communist and this was bad. This contention delayed Chicano organizing for more than ten years.

Most Chicanas knew more about Ricky Ricardo and Lucy from the "I Love Lucy Show." Some paid attention to Ronald Reagan in *Bedtime for Bonzo*, but most were not impressed. After the Korean conflict, the G.I. Bill once again made it possible for men to go to college, purchase houses, and acquire small business loans. This created a greater economic and political gap between men and women, leaving most women in positions of having abandoned rural environments for urban lifestyles, and highly dependent on men. When President Dwight D. Eisenhower took office in 1953, the Rosenbergs were executed in the electric chair. They had been convicted of selling atomic secrets to the Soviet Union. Richard Nixon was the vice president, and Marilyn Monroe was the latest Hollywood "blond bombshell." She became the most powerful symbol of feminine beauty in the world, but Chicanas were physically unable to meet that standard of beauty. Some bleached their hair, but their skin was still brown.

In 1954, after years of struggle, African Americans were successful in beginning a national desegregation effort in the form of a Supreme Court ruling known as the *Brown v. the Board of Education* decision. This decision maintained that separate educational facilities for whites and people of color were inherently unequal. The Court followed this decision with a directive that school boards integrate "with all deliberate speed." The U.S. Civil Rights Commission set up offices in the Southwest, and complaints of discrimination were slowly investigated, documented, and sometimes corrected.

In 1955, a black woman named Rosa Parks refused to rise from her seat on a bus so that a white man could sit. When she refused to ride at the back of the Montgomery, Alabama, bus, the civil rights movement was ignited and was hurled into national attention. Chicanos, however, were busy gaining cultural and racial consciousness. When Chicanas finally got to the university, in the early 1970s, they were subjected to eurocentric, male-dominated theories that were developed in the 1950s. These theories included a consensus framework maintaining that the social values of racial or ethnic minorities would converge with dominant values over time and that assimilation of people of color would take place (Parsons, 1951). This model did not take into consideration the viciousness of a racist social system that entraps people of color into positions of powerlessness. In fact, this hierarchical social structure deters assimilation by imposing phenomenal social costs due to the suppression of resources that could be contributed by people of color, especially women. This theory is not about consensus because it does not explain how those in power do not want to relinquish that power.

The interdependence theorists contended that ethnic groups would interact and cooperate regardless of unshared values in order to make social gains (Durkheim, 1964). The passage of thirty to forty years has revealed this to be untrue. People of color will not trade cultural identity because they need certain things. In fact, they will become more resistant. The theory renders a depiction of racial and ethnic groups as desperate, willing to give up salient survival mechanisms in order to get a piece of the American Dream. The theory neglected to note that conquered people do not so easily give up their culture, especially when they have witnessed the abuse of their people over the course of a lifetime.

Struggle is a central theme among Chicanas. The conflict theorists view conflict and coercion as central features of adapting to a social structure. Adaptation is necessary for change (Coser, 1959; Dahrendorf, 1959). Chicanos have changed; in fact, they have bent with the economic and political times for one and one half centuries. The conflict model beats the racial or ethnic community into either going along with the social plan or enduring the consequences of not conforming. In this model, conflict will evolve to produce a call for revolution, the overthrow of the capitalist system, and the emergence of a classless society. This contention offers a radical resolution that appealed to Chicanos of the 1960s and

1970s. The overthrow of the oppressive capitalist system was an ideal for some, as was the emergence of a society without divisions. The idea was attractive to the many disenfranchised people of various backgrounds in the 1960s. The attraction was red baited, and most U.S. citizens never found out that the attraction had less to do with communism and more to do with a dislike for a hierarchically structured, male-dominated, capitalist society.

Chicano youth of the 1960s underestimated the practicality of the ideology, but not for long. They quickly realized that the disenfranchised did not control the resources; rather, the white owners of the means of production and the white government controlled the resources, and would utilize them against anyone who threatened the establishment. Conflict theorists did not perceive the world as consensual or stable. Competition was a key factor. Academic women and scholars of color extended that racism, and sexism limited competition primarily to white males. The youth needed radical change; they needed release from the limitations of their racial, class, and gender roles in society. In the mid-1990s, the Los Angeles trial of athlete, actor, and spokesperson O. J. Simpson brought to national attention the intersection of class, racism, and sexism in the criminal justice system. In the 1960s, however, confrontation, tension, and conflict became the leading model of social change and cultural preservation for Chicanos.

In the 1960s, few Chicanas attended university, but not all learning and advocacy were taking place in class. Before that decade, few Chicanas had gotten published. Thus, few textbooks recounted their experience. Cleofas Jaramillo, author of *Romance of a Little Village Girl* (1955); *Cuentos del Hogar* (1939); and *Shadows of the Past/Sombras del Pasado* (1941) wrote about traditional culture. Fabiola Cabeza de Baca, *We Fed Them Cactus* (1954), also documented traditional stories and customs. These women produced extensive reflections on women's life before the coming of the Anglo, and how it changed after they came. Cabeza de Baca even joined the New Mexico Folklore Society in an effort to promote cultural saliency and survival for contemporary Chicanos. By the late 1960s, Chicanas were writing their own stories about the transition from field to factory, urbanization, and colonization via activist poetry and position papers on the movement. Chicanas were working, thinking, and talking in their homes, the fields, factories, and government offices. Some students were strongly influenced by the writing of Franz Fannon (1963) and Albert Memmi (1965). Most were influenced by the most important people in their immediate lives: their grandmothers. Without being theoretical, all focused on the intersection of color, class, and gender. Few men encouraged Chicana feminist consciousness raising, and unfortunately, remnants of these early divisions are still felt. But when women entered the arena of linking theory to practice, the Chicano community took on another dimension, one that was more concerned with the daily lives of all its people.

The academic dimension extended internal colonialism as a model that still permeates Chicana and Chicano activism. Internal colonialism is an extension of Marx's class analysis and his work on capitalistic imperialism (1955) to include racism. It also extends the words of Robert Blauner (1969) on white imperialism within the United States. Various elements of race relations theories are incorporated in the model that dominates Chicano Studies, the academic arm of the movement. This perspective maintains that racial prejudice is largely a product of racial ideologies that were developed to justify conquering Mexicans and imposing structural discrimination. In other words, discrimination against Chicanos exists because racist thoughts and beliefs are maintained and practiced.

CHICANA POLITICAL CONSCIOUSNESS

By the late 1960s, the cold war had been exposed by American youth as U.S. nationalist propaganda. By the 1970s, activist Chicanas had overcome this brainwashing, and feminist thoughts had extended into action maintaining that the United States and males were not always right. They no longer believed that there was freedom and justice for all; that they lived in the greatest country in the world just because it was the richest; and that they should be contented women in the lowest status of all in a stratified social structure. More poetry, more nonelectoral position papers, and more academic papers, even books, began to appear on the subject of sexism.

In the 1980s, the movement became more conforming as a result of Republican presidential rule. Advocating change within the system's structure, from within, was the model of activism. Chicanas did not conform when they infiltrated the system. They pushed their feminist agenda to empower women in the departments of the university, at the student meetings, in government offices, and in the community. The conformist focus was on understanding the process by which people win and lose in a hierarchical structured society. The emphasis was on entering the structure, surviving within it, and changing it from within. The major criticism of this approach was that it was too slow and that only a few individuals benefited. Basically, the model assumed that there are components within the structure of U.S. society which have the specific function and goal of allowing people to participate. If Chicanos played their "minority" role correctly in the society, the society would continue with stability and harmony. In the true order model of academia, gradual change is achieved through society's adaptation to the new social needs of its people. The role of the Chicanos with internal positions is to ensure the direction of the change by outmoding structures, like discrimination, from within.

When Leticia Sotero Vasquez was beaten by a twenty-five-year male veteran of the Riverside sheriff's office, the complacency of the 1980s that had been lamented by activist Chicanos came to an end. Latinos in southern California became more united in resisting racist immigration and affirmative action policy. They were more united against the 1980s approach to social change that had pitted Chicano and other Latino groups against one another, and the intelligentsia arm of the movement included women who played a prominent role.

Between the 1960s and late 1990s Chicano Studies had been conceptualized, developed, and implemented. Even though its existence is a continuous struggle, today there are classes on Chicanas, their role in the family, art, and public policy. Some of the 1960s students who founded and developed Chicano Studies still teach in the discipline. In the beginning, activist scholars were concentrated in the social sciences and education, and some scholars in modern languages teaching Spanish tended to be cultural preservationists. Chicanas in history, politics, sociology, economics, and anthropology took from their disciplines what was salient and moved in a Chicana Studies direction that was radically different from the traditional disciplines.

In Chicana Studies they confront contemporary stereotypes, They no longer live down to a standard, serving a passive homogeneous group of women with a single, Mexican-American heritage rooted in conquest and raised in a farm worker background. They are scholars, attorneys, doctors, social workers, and biochemists.

When Chicanas first became involved in the civil rights movement, their goal was to openly confront discrimination, correct historical conflicts, and seek retribution. They joined these efforts in a variety of elements, including education, politics, the criminal justice system, art, the church, health, employment and economics, and housing. At the university, Chicanas studied how the Spanish conquistadores had come to the New World in search of gold and glory in the name of their God. They sought to reconquer their world spiritually, physically, psychologically, socially, and politically (Blea, 1995). Because the Anglo had conquered the Southwest assuming they were under the guidance of their God, Chicanas began to criticize not only the white-dominated Catholic Church, but also the male-centered God of Christianity and the proposed immaculate conception of the Virgin Mary. Instead, they focused on Aztec and Mayan spirituality and on what had happened to it because of war and conquest. They questioned why they had not learned about them in school, in church, or in their home. Chicanas have indeed redefined themselves.

Feminist Chicanas emerged out of the 1950s and 1960s artistry of Elvis

Presley love songs, the Beatles, and Janis Joplin. Like their white counterparts, they gave up wanting to be a princess like actress Grace Kelly, who abandoned her movie career to marry a monarch. Instead, they began to burn incense and sympathize with the global struggles of oppressed people everywhere. On their home TVs, they saw black women trying to go to school in spite of the ugly names and violence hurled at them by white women and men. At the movies they saw Rita Moreno dance and sing in *West Side Story*. It didn't matter whether she was Puerto Rican or Cuban. She was a Latina and La Chicana recognized her, her desires, the barrio she lived in, and the men around her. La Chicana was young, impressionable, and confident that she did not want an Anglo boyfriend as Maria did in the movie, but she wanted what she thought he could provide: food, clothes, vacations, two children, and PTA (Parent Teacher Association) meetings.

In the movies Latina actresses like Dolores del Rio (Lolita Dolores Martinez Asunsolo Lopez Negrete) changed their names and played the "dark lady," the sultry, sneaky vamp. María Montez, Lupe Velez, and Kathy Jurado kept their Latino names, but some had to change their names to Anglo names. Rita Hayworth was originally Rita Cansino. Raquel Welch was originally Raquel Tejada. It took several years to find out that Lynda Carter of the television series "Wonder Woman," Catherine Bach of "The Dukes of Hazard," and Victoria Principal of "Dallas" were Latinas. Other Latina actresses include Elizabeth Pena, Rachel Ticotin, Roana de Soto, María Conchita Alonso, Daphne Zuniga, Norma Aleandro, and Linda Cristal. Both the feminist and Chicano movements have even motivated independent art film producers like Lourdes Protillo and Solome Espana to engage in experimental films.

Chicana feminist consciousness raising took place at the university, but it also occurred at organizing meetings where the Chicanas viewed a 16-millimeter film entitled *Salt of the Earth*. They learned that the movie, which was among the first to note the intersection of race, class, and gender, had been "blackballed" or "blacklisted" by members of the U.S. government. The actors could not work in Hollywood, where ex-President Reagan cooperated with the effort. The leading actress was deported to Mexico, but from the movie the Chicanas learned that women had power. As girls, if they had resources, they pin-curled their hair, played with hoola-hoops, wore petticoats, and bought 45 rpm recordings of La Bamba by Chicano Ritchie Valens; they wore Max Factor lipstick and powder, Evening in Paris cologne that they bought in beautiful blue bottles at the local Woolworth store. In the 1960s the Chicana washed her hair and face clean, removed the mask of colonialism, and put on a pair of working man's jeans and a halter top. She combed her hair long and loose, made protest signs, and went out to demonstrate. Gone were the illusions of the many Barbie dolls she never possessed, the teddy bear she never hugged, the dream car, the dream house, and the dream man who was going to buy it all. She came to embrace the fact that Chicana mothers gave birth with little medical attention, and endured poverty even though their fathers and mothers worked long, hard hours.

They did not want their mother's life, nor did they want to die in industrial accidents, as their fathers had. Chicanas reinvented themselves within the context of debates on the use of birth control pills. This took place first within the frameworks of their minds, their churches, and then their bedrooms. The issue filtered into their communities among other Mexican-American women, and finally into the Chicano movement as part of a political platform that was not supported by both men and some women. Not even the forced sterilization of Puerto Rican and Mexican-American women was protested. The pill was slow to become available in the barrio. Chicanas shyly asked Anglo male doctors to prescribe them. They balanced feeling guilty, sinful, and dirty, while on television they watched Russia beat the United States in the 1960 Olympics in Rome, Italy. All this time, Chicana feminist consciousness was building. They took the pill, endured its side effects, and ventured outside of prescribed gender roles to help the farm workers and to get John F. Kennedy elected. As their political consciousness grew, most family members were highly displeased.

Chicanas were interested in the Olympics not because Chicanas were athletic enthusiasts but for political reasons. Some Chicanas had joined study groups where they analyzed the Communist Manifesto of Karl Marx (1955). Others studied China and the teachings of Mao. Few joined the Communist Workers party or the Socialist Workers party. Instead, they became active in what was considered the radical August 29th movement, which later became the League of Revolutionary Struggle. When Chicanas applauded the Russians during the Olympics, not all did so because they loved, or even truthfully understood, male competitive cultures or the ramifications of communist politics and ideology. They cheered more because they disliked the power of the United States. The defeat put it in its place and diminished its facade of freedom and justice for all in front of the whole world. In this context, we should not forget that this was done within a social framework in which the movie *Salt of the Earth* had been red baited. This Hollywood production addressed the issues of race, class, and gender, and was red baited when the U.S. Representatives' House UnAmerican Activities Committee sought to identify and remove communist sympathizers from American society. The safe victory of the Russians over the United States neutralized the power of the oppressor of people of color all over the world, if even for a short while. When Wilma Randolph set a record in the 100 meter final and Cassius Clay (Muhammad Ali) outboxed competitors at the Olympics,

Chicanas recognized that they and their fellow African Americans had a common oppressor.

While the movement continued, some Mexican-American women still teased their bleached hair into beehive hairdos and sprayed it stiff. These women still wanted to be like "Jackie," who was rich and married to the rich young man who had grown up to be the president of the United States. In short, many Chicanas had internalized the American Dream for women. This dream was difficult to extinguish in spite of the fact that the reality was that most of them were poor or working class, at best. They tended to be "barrioized" urban dwellers in segregated communities of crowded housing. Many were still rural. Dolores Huerta rode to national prominence in the 1960s and 1970s after having been part of the founding of the United Farm Workers. Huerta was born in Raton, New Mexico, but for years worked with Cesar Chavez. Helen Chavez endured hardship because of Cesar's politics. With minimal education she managed the farm workers' credit union. Personal conversations with Dolores Huerta reveal that she regrets not organizing the women. (This regret was also revealed in an October 1995 radio interview on KPFK, Los Angeles, with John Martinez.)

According to popular estimates, 42 percent of California's population joined the grape boycott at its height. The United Farm Workers (UFW) also had supporters all over the nation. Robert and Ethel Kennedy joined the effort, and Joan Baez sang, "No, no, no nos moveran . . . (we shall not be moved)." Chicanas wore handkerchiefs tied behind their heads, and participated in rallies and fund raisers, where cries of "Chicano, Chicano, Chicano Power!" were heard across the nation. A long UFW strike in 1965 had picketers chanting "Viva la Huelga" ("Long Live the Strike") on national TV. Negative national publicity forced dozens of agricultural growers to bargain with the UFW. The U.S. civil rights movement, which included the Vietnam protest and the feminist movement, frightened university administrators and government officials into granting financial aid so that poor people of color could attend the universities. The UFW plight was aligned with broader movement concerns, such as demands for better public education, political representation, health care, and justice in the criminal justice system.

Chicana parents feared for their daughters' safety and reputation and wondered what the "girls" were doing "out there" protesting. They might get hurt or even raped. A few young women did get hurt; some went to jail, and others got tear gassed. Some experimented with marijuana, a few with LSD, and most with sex. As liberals and clergy flocked to support the UFW, they inadvertently supported the Chicano movement. In 1966, more than 50,000 protestors marched from Delano, California, to Sacramento during Easter Week, the holiest week in the Christian calendar. Chicanas joined the national grape boycott and picketed supermarkets. Later they picketed and boycotted lettuce. These

efforts cost agricultural growers millions of dollars and kept giving motivation to the movement. Chicanas learned that organizing in the fields
went back to the 1930s and 1940s. By 1975, the UFW had 50 contracts in
the grape industry alone, and hundreds of Chicano community advocacy
groups were thriving around the country. During this time, China was
rapidly increasing its agricultural production through a huge industrial
movement that had begun in 1972. The country's oldest problem was
the lack of enough food. Large pig farms and tractor plants gave evidence to the movement. Another movement was one that sought to bring
China into contemporary international competition without destroying
its culture.

A POLICY PERSPECTIVE

The farm worker movement may have gotten the most media attention, but the media did not miss the fact that Chicanos in Tierra Amarilla,
New Mexico, had attacked the county courthouse with guns and rifles
on June 15, 1967. This was the result of a struggle over ancestral homelands granted by Mexico and Spain to their citizens during the colonial
period. Land rights were guaranteed to Mexicanos by Americanos via
the Treaty of Guadalupe Hidalgo. In the summer of 1967, however, tanks
and soldiers terrorized women, children, and the elderly as they invaded
the small mountain village looking for the attackers. Patsy Tijerina was
especially targeted. Her husband, Reyes Lopez Tijerina, led the courthouse raid. Patsy set a U.S. Forest Service sign on fire and thereby got
national media attention. Several others burned the Forest Service signs
during the Kit Carson National Forest occupation. Patsy was convicted
and placed on five years' probation for civil disobedience (Acuna, 1988;
Gomez-Quinones, 1990).

In 1968, thousands of students from predominantly Mexican-American
high schools in east Los Angeles walked out of school in an event that
became known as the Blow Outs. Basically, this educational reform
movement tied educational problems to life in the urban barrios where
high unemployment, poor housing, and inferior medical care were the
norm. Students and their adult supporters formulated "21 Demands,"
which included a Chicano curriculum, upgraded facilities, better teachers, and career counseling. In this case, California law was used crea-
tively. The protestors sought to deny schools monetary support for each
day a student was absent from school. This made the walkouts most
effective, and like the grape boycott, this event taught Chicanas that people will respond when they are embarrassed and when they are losing
money. Thirteen leaders were arrested on charges of conspiring to dis-
turb the peace. Among them was a teacher named Sal Castro, who was
fired and who got most of the attention. But there were hundreds of
women who participated in meetings, picket lines, and street demon-

strations. Some women "sat-in" at the Los Angeles School Board room until Castro was reinstated and a Mexican-American Advisory Board was created.

Across the Southwest and the country at large, Chicanas struggled to organize, to go to meetings, and to plan strategy, but they were invisible as a group. They were among those who protested the invasion of the Bay of Pigs in 1961 and were on Fidel Castro's side. They danced the twist, and they painfully watched their brothers aspire to be Green Berets during the war in Vietnam. When the Freedom Riders were attacked in 1961 in the South, they got angry, and some Chicanas noticed something called the Alliance for Progress, where the United States and nineteen Latin American nations signed a charter creating a ten-year economic effort backed by $20 million in long-term financing from the United States to Latin American countries. Cuba dissented. U.S. intervention was protested by Chicanas, but their voice was not yet loud enough.

At this time, the United States was beginning its efforts in outer space. Martin Luther King, Jr., gave his "I Have a Dream" speech at the largest civil rights demonstration ever held in the United States. Some Chicanas were there as students. When our younger brothers got killed in Vietnam, Chicanas got downright mad. This anger was quelled when it was realized that Anglos killed their own at Kent State and when John F. Kennedy was shot in the head and died. We watched the assassination tape play and replay and replay yet again on television, and we grew fearful. If they could do this to one of their own, what would they do to us?

It did not take us long to find out. Race riots soon became a common occurrence. The Civil Rights Act was passed on July 3, 1964, setting up several measures and agencies to combat racism in the United States. The first Chicanas to get work outside of domestic, farm, or factory work got jobs during Johnson's War on Poverty. It made federal money available for a variety of social programs like legal aid for the poor, Head Start for poor children, and student financial aid. The War on Poverty created nonelectoral political involvement and social awareness that allowed women of color to participate. In 1964, the Economic Opportunity Act was passed and administered via the Office of Economic Opportunity (OEO). This created new job training agencies like Job Corps, Head Start, Upward Bound, and Vista. A few women, like Solema Vallejo-Neary of Denver, Colorado, went to other countries. Vallejo-Neary received a presidential award from the president of Costa Rica for teaching women, men, and children how to farm. Other women learned to manage and teach in Head Start.

Many investigations were effective as a result of federal intervention in poverty and poor race relations. In Albuquerque, New Mexico, in March 1966, the causes for the disproportionate number of U.S. unemployed and educated Chicanos were explored. Most meetings like this failed to achieve much more then ventilation of grievances. Chicanas and Chicanos both protested at microphones, learned to confront the federal and state authorities, and walked out of meetings. Special task forces and committees were established, which often pitted Chicano against Chicano. Women such as Priscilla Mares in El Paso, Hercelia Toscano in San Antonio, Delia Villegas in Chicago, Dominga G. Coronado and Patricia Jaquez in La Junta, Colorado, and Faustina Solis in Berkeley, California, advocated for their communities in the areas of education, mental health, vocational training, and employment while calling for the unity of raza.

The war in Vietnam escalated as Chicanas listened to the music of the Rolling Stones, the Beatles, and Santana. Tex Mex music, however, never faded in popularity. Chicanas mourned as their brothers came home in body bags, and they went to funeral after funeral.

Some Chicanos participated in the California Watts Riots on August 16, 1965, but the nation did not know about it. The media presented the riot solely as a black–white issue.

As soldiers were reported "missing in action," the National Organization for Women (NOW) asserted feminism with more vigor. Chicanas addressed the issues within their own movement, severely limiting contact with NOW. Race riots increased in places like Atlanta and Chicago, and at the same time, an important piece of legislation carrying a Latino surname emerged. "You have the right to remain silent. Anything you say may be used against you in a court of law. . . ." The Miranda Act passed on June 13, 1966. It granted suspects civil liberties and protection from self-incrimination. The police officer who did not inform the suspect of his or her rights was in violation of the law. The act is named after Ernest Miranda of Arizona, who had been charged with rape.

During this time, women wore miniskirts, bell bottoms, and halter tops for the first time in public. Cassius Clay had renamed himself Muhammad Ali, flower children sprang up, and millions of Americans were shedding old traditions. Dr. Benjamin Spock was arrested for protesting the war in Vietnam and trying to shut down an Army induction center in New York in 1967. Labor leaders opposed the war, Martin Luther King Jr., was murdered on April 4, 1968, and Robert Kennedy was killed two months later. Chicanas saw that those who sought to change society could and would be killed. Chicano youth at east Los Angeles high schools held the blowouts. In March 1968, 10,000 students from five east Los Angeles schools protested inferior education by walking out. The 50 percent educational dropout rate was seen as a pushout rate. Students were pushed out by the irrelevancy of the curriculum. Students, like those in Denver, also walked out around the country.

In 1968, university and college campuses were ablaze with student activity. Chicanas and Chicanos protested Coors beer on campus. At the same time, technology had finally crept into Chicano homes, and the adults, as well as the youth, were watching television along with the rest of the world, when, on August 29, 1968, it was reported that approximately 10,000 protesting white youths were at the Democratic Convention in Chicago. A confrontation between the police and the youths resulted in the spilling of blood as officers beat up the white youths.

CIVIL DISOBEDIENCE

Other acts of civil disobedience and protest took place. The Brown Berets, founded by David Sanchez on December 3, 1967, were the largest Chicano student organization, with nationwide membership of 5,000 young women and men in more than 80 chapters. Sanchez founded the Chicano Moratorium Committee to protest the Vietnam War and its overrepresentation of Chicano casualties. Sanchez had a brother in Vietnam. The march brought an estimated 30,000 people to Whittier Boulevard in east Los Angeles on August 29, 1970. It turned violent. There were riots, and Ruben Salazar, a well-respected journalist, was shot. The Brown Berets were male dominated and had militaristic tactics; they organized to oppose the militaristic practices of the police and sheriff's office. Brown Beret women did not shy away from militarism during the Moratorium, nor did they during the time that Pauline Mendoza and others visited the Brown Beret-occupied Santa Catalina Island in California. Part of the occupation team included Maria Blanco, who was left behind with her husband Jeronimo when the group was forced to disband on November 1, 1972.

U.S. racism gained international attention in October 1972 when black solidarity protesting the treatment of blacks in the United States was displayed at the Olympics in Mexico City (*Chronicle of America*, 1983). Fueling the heated times was the televised image of an executed Vietcong officer on February 1. With a single shot to the head, the officer's head exploded at the end of a gun. Chicanas shivered, as did women throughout the world. The man whose brain spread across the TV screens and across the front pages of newspapers was someone's son, someone's brother; so was the one who pulled the trigger.

In the struggle to liberate themselves, Chicanas studied communism and socialism, and discovered patriarchal societies. They analyzed revolutions in Mexico, Russia, Cuba, and China for guidance, and found liberation role models in Che and Fidel Castro, as well as Chairman Mao. Female models were hard to find, and so Chicanas found themselves inventing their liberation. They were their own role models. In March 1969, during the Easter weekend, over 1,500 mostly young men and women gathered in Denver, Colorado, for the first Chicano Youth Liberation Conference sponsored by the Crusade for Justice. The youth conference was organized primarily by women in the wake of the northern New Mexico, Tierra Amarilla land struggle. Among the organizers was Rodolfo "Corky" Gonzalez, who had been a boxer and an activist in the region for some time. The real work was done communally. Among the workers were Jerri and Anita Gonzales, Betita Martinez, Juanita Dominguez, Precilla Salazar, and Marcella Lucero Trujillo (1975). The conference examined the social and economic plight of urban Mexican Americans. The name "Chicano" was adopted as a self-defining concept, and not just as a label.

The Plan del Espiritu de Aztlan defined cultural nationalism, not communism or socialism, as the ideological framework of the movement. The plan was based on an Aztec legend (see Chapter 2), which defined the national homeland as Aztlan. It was at this conference that Chicano issues first gained a national platform. After this conference, they were no longer treated as a passing conversation. In fact, there was a major split at the conference over feminist concerns. Some of the Crusade for Justice women, who were hosting the conference, decided that feminism was not in their nationalist interest and influenced the conference until a decision against Chicana feminism was rendered. The apparent defeat brought more women into the discussion, and the small number of women at the conference gained many more supporters. Some Chicana feminists condemned the conference as sexist (Enriquez and Mirande, 1979). I called Nita Gonzales and later went to see her father, Corky, about feminist issues. They stressed la familia as a model for the movement. They did not want to create friction between males and females. Later, the women at the conference changed their position.

Chicanas began to organize small groups of women criticizing the movement, especially its male dominance, but issues of sexism were still not being confronted in community meetings across Aztlan as part of the overall agenda. Racism, not sexism, was the central issue in Crystal City, Texas, a small city of 10,000 people dominated by the Del Monte agricultural and food processing corporation. In this city, only one Mexican-American cheerleader per year was allowed to participate in school events. This was a city with 10,000 Mexican-American inhabitants, roughly 80 percent of the population. A protest challenging the high school practice escalated into action founding La Raza Unida party. Among the founders and activists of the party are Luz Gutierrez, Martha Cotera, and Rosie Castro. La Raza Unida and one of its leaders, Jose Angel Gutierrez, challenged the two-party system by severely splitting it and charging it with being racist. The party grew beyond Crystal City, producing monumental educational reform in south Texas, especially, with the assistance of the U.S. Department of Justice. From this event,

Chicanas learned to use the law and other public policy to achieve objectives or gain some opportunity for change.

Richard M. Nixon became president of the United States in 1968 amid much talk about loss of funding support for programs addressing ethnic and racial inequities in the United States. By the time Woodstock took place and Neil Armstrong walked on the moon on July 24, 1969, women had gained extensive experience protesting and getting media attention. As the Nixon administration advanced, however, many of the earlier gains by poor people were lost.

It is difficult to criticize a movement that so profoundly affected Latinos in the United States. Chicanas shaped the movement and gained valuable experience in both electoral and nonelectoral politics. Chicana feminism did not erupt spontaneously, nor did it evolve in everyone in the same direction. Some female consciousness developed faster than others. In fact, it is still in the process of developing. Not all Chicana/ Latina feminists agree on everything in the same manner. As is true of other progressive movements, the feminist movement is rather diverse.

By the time male leaders like Corky Gonzales, Jose Angel Gutierrez, and Reyes Tijerina were speaking to students about urban issues and organizing la Raza Unida party and the land rights struggle, Chicanas were linking theory to practice in terms of the movement being a people's movement. They were people, and they thought their concerns should be addressed by the movement, which excluded them from being involved in the leadership and policy-making process.

Education was a primary concern, but sexism was not an issue for Chicano educational activists who were advocating bilingual education. It rarely arises as an issue in bilingual education today. In the 1970s, only three of ten Chicanos twenty-five years of age and over had completed at least four years of high school (U.S. Bureau of the Census, 1993). Less than one in twenty had completed four years or more of college. Progress was very slow. By 1980, about four in ten Hispanos/Chicanos had completed four years or more of high school, and one of every thirteen had completed four years of college or more.

Chicanas were active in both electoral and nonelectoral politics. Nationalism, centering on Chicano culture and ethnicity, was the dominant thread in Chicano politics. During this time, the Raza Unida party and the Crusade for Justice were perhaps the most nationalistic Chicano political organizations. The party's seeds were planted at the Cabinet Committee Hearings in October 1967 in El Paso, Texas. It sought to work within the dominant political structure by changing the color of its face, by involving more Chicanos at the organizing levels, and by supporting the election of Chicano candidates. The nationalistic movement heavily influenced Chicano politics throughout the United States in a way that still can be felt today. Although few adhere to a purely nationalistic ideology, it cannot be denied that most, if not all, Chicano political activity has taken this form of activity to some degree or another.

Martha Cotera wrote *Diosa y Hembra* (1976), the first Chicana textbook distributed nationally. At the same time, Marcella Lucero Trujillo advocated prison reform and Chicano Studies in Denver. She later left to work on one of the first Chicana Ph.D.s in Chicana literature. I met her when she invited me to read poetry for the Cinco de Mayo which she also organized in Minnesota. Chicanas began to have their own conferences, primarily on university campuses, but the community was always a viable part of their agenda.

In the community, Elizabeth Martinez and Enriqueta Longeaux y Vasquez published a movement newspaper in New Mexico, *El Grito Del Norte* (The Cry of the North). A Chicana feminist journal, *Encuentro Femenil*, was followed by *Regeneration*, first published in east Los Angeles in 1971, through the hard work of Francisca Flores. The publications featured articles on stereotypes, Chicana feminist studies, and organizations such as the Comision Femenil Mexicana Nacional, which was established in order to organize and train women to take leadership roles. The Comision held its first meeting in 1970.

All over the country Chicana activists were linking their ideology to their own lives. Alicia Escalante was instrumental in creating the Welfare Rights Organization. Lupe Anguiano, a former nun, developed the Bilingual Education Act. Maria Hernández, a founding member of La Raza Unida party in Texas, was still active in 1977, when the women of Crystal City met to address their own issues, and I had hosted the first Chicana Conference in Boulder, Colorado (Blea, 1995). At this time, other women in other parts of the country were having their own conferences and their own confrontations. Many of these confrontations were hostile. One woman, Anna Nieto-Gomez, resisted Chicano sexism in the Department of Chicano Studies at California State University, Northridge. She and other activist Chicanas like Lea Yberra, Ines Talamantes, Inez Hernandes, Ada Sosa-Riddel, and Margaritta Melville wrote their own poetry, articles, and books at the same time they mentored other Chicanas. Anna Nieto-Gomez was ousted from the campus and proceeded with her work in the community, but not before she addressed their sexism. In the community not far from Nieto-Gomez, Chicana scholar Linda Apodaca was researching the women of the Community Service Organization.

The first Chicana feminist conference appears to have been held in Houston, Texas, in May 1971. The theme of the conference did not apparently separate women's issues from men's: Las Mujeres por La Raza. The most controversial workshops were on sexuality, abortion, and birth control. A year later, La Raza Unida party held its first national convention. Chicanas had their own caucus. Research on the reaction to these efforts must be conducted. After I had hosted the 1977 Chicana Conferences, where there were panel presentations on feminism, my home was attacked in the middle of the night. My picture window was broken, the phone kept ringing, and my four-year-old daughter was terrorized. Among the terrorists were other Chicanas.

Chicana feminists entered into power struggles with men and women resisting feminism, but they also witnessed power struggles among the men, especially during 1970, and at the Raza Unida political convention, where Chicanos had gathered to nominate a candidate for U.S. president. At the convention there appeared to be room for only one leader. It was the structure of Anglo-dominated politics that fragmented the effort, and so Chicana feminists did not want to contribute to it. The one-leader approach was inappropriate, they thought; the effort to self-govern had to be communal. But no one heard this message. The men kept on giving speeches that their female colleagues, sisters, girlfriends, and wives had written for them. This defeated the Chicana objective of collectivity. At fund raisers the women got up early to cook the food. They worked all day selling it while the men talked. At the end of the day, the women cleaned up, and the men picked up the crumbled dollar bills and sweaty change the women had spent all day collecting. The men took control of the money physically and on paper. At meetings, these males reported that "we" had raised a certain amount of money. Women finally noted, after much discussion with other women, that they were the ones who did the hard work, and they wanted to talk about concerns relevant to them, to children, and to men. The men laughed, trivializing the effort, calling female political dialogue *comadriando* (gossip). There was always some man who suggested the group thank the women for their fund raising efforts by giving them applause. Some women were content. Others let it be known that they were not satisfied with applause; they wanted to be respected. They wanted to be part of the decision-making process. They wanted to impact movement policy.

REFERENCES

Acuna, Rodolfo. 1988. *Occupied America: A History of Chicanos.* 3rd ed. New York: Harper and Row.

Baez, Joan, 1966. *Daybreak.* New York: Avon.

Blauner, Robert. 1969. "Internal Colonialism and Ghetto Revolt." *Social Problems* 16 (Spring): 393–408.

Blea, Irene I. 1991. *Bessemer: A Sociological Perspective of a Chicano Barrio.* New York: AMS Press.

———. 1995. *Researching Chicano Communities: Social-Historical, Physical, Psychological, and Spiritual Space.* New York: Praeger.

Cabeza de Baca, Fabiola. 1954. *We Fed Them Cactus.* Albuquerque: University of New Mexico Press.

Coser, Lewis A. 1959. *The Function of Social Conflict*. Glencoe, Ill.: Free Press.

Cotera, Martha. 1976. *Diosa y Hembra*. Austin, Tex.: Information Systems Development.

Chronicle of America. 1993. Mount Kisco, N.Y.: Chronicle Publications.

Dahrendorf, Ralf. 1959. *Class and Class Conflict in Industrial Society*. Stanford, Calif.: Stanford University Press.

Durkheim, Emile. 1915. *The Elementary Forms of the Religious Life*. New York: Macmillan and Free Press. (Originally published in 1897.)

————. 1964. *The Division of Labor in Society*. Translated by George Simpson. New York: Macmillan and Free Press. (Originally published in 1893.)

Enriquez, Evangelina, and Alfredo Mirande. 1979. *La Chicana: The Mexican-American Woman*. Chicago: University of Illinois Press.

Fannon, Franz. 1963. *The Wretched of the Earth*. New York: Grove Press, 1963.

Garcia, John, Julia Curry Rodriguez, and Clara Lomas, eds. 1988. *Times of Challenge: Chicanos and Chicanas in American Society*. Houston: University of Houston Press, Mexican American Studies Program, Monograph Series No. 6.

Gomez-Quinones, Juan. 1990a. "Chicano Politics." *La Raza Magazine*, Vol. 2. Albuquerque: University of New Mexico Press, pp. 115–118.

————1990b. "Patsy Tijerina on Suspended Sentence, But It's Our Land." *La Raza Magazine*, Vol. 2, p. 58.

Heller, Celia. 1966. *Mexican American Youth: Forgotten Youth at the Crossroads*. New York: Random House.

Hernández, Deluvina. 1970. *Mexican American Challenge to a Sacred Cow*. Los Angeles: Chicano Cultural Center.

Jaramillo, Cleofas. 1939. *Cuentos del Hogar*. El Campo, Tex.: Citizen Press. Reprinted 1942. Santa Fe, N. Mex.: Seton Village Press.

————. 1941. *Sombras del Pasado/ Shadows of the Past*. Santa Fe:, N. Mex.: Ancient City Press.

————. 1955. *Romance of a Little Village Girl*. San Antonio, Tex.: Naylor.

Kluckhohn, Florence, and Fred L. Strodbeck. 1961. *Variations in Value Orientations*. Evanston, Ill.: Row Peterson.

Lammana, Richard, and Julian Samora. 1967. *Mexican Americans in a Midwest Metropolis: A Study of East Chicago*. Los Angeles: Mexican American Project.

Marx, Karl, and Friedrich Engels. 1955. *Communist Manifesto*. Chicago: H. Regnery Co.

Marx, Karl, and Friedrich Engels. 1965. "The Communist Manifesto." In Arthur Mendel, ed., *Essential Works of Marxism*. New York: Bantam Books. (Original work published in 1848.)

Madsen, William. 1964. *Mexican Americans of South Texas*. New York: Holt, Rinehart and Winston.

Melville, Margaritta B. 1980. *Twice a Minority*. St. Louis: C. V. Mosby Press.

Memmi, Albert. 1965. *The Colonizer and the Colonized*. Boston: Beacon Press.

Parsons, Talcott. 1951. *Essays on Sociological Theory*. Glencoe, Ill.: Free Press.

Romano, Octavio. 1968. "The Anthropology and Sociology of the Mexican Americans: The Distortion of Mexican-American History." *El Grito* (Fall).

Trujillo, Marcella Lucero. 1975, March 12–16. "The Road to Canon: The Road to La Pinta." *An Anthology of Chicano Literature*. Austin: Chicano Studies Center.

Tuck, Ruth. 1946. *Not with the Fist: Mexican Americans in a Southwest City.* New York: Harcourt, Brace and Co.

U.S. Department of Commerce, Economics and Statistics Administration, Bureau of the Census. 1993, November. *We the American Hispanics.* Washington, D.C.: Government Printing Office. p. 8.

9

DECENTRALIZING WHITE PATRIARCHY

On the trip to China some women reported that the men in their lives were extremely supportive of their attendance, but there seemed to be difficulty with others. Some had fights with their husbands and lovers just before they left. Most had to call home periodically. Others had insufficient funds or worried about "other women" entering their husbands' lives while they were away.

In the U.S. press, there was an outcry of resistance from powerful political men who feared what women would do in China. Reverend James Dobson, an influential religious leader with many political connections, warned that the U.N. conference was the greatest threat to the family he had ever encountered in his lifetime (Snortland, 1995). In addition, a "Focus on the Family" conference held in Denver, Colorado, in 1995 covered the following topics that were apparently threatening to men: women starving, epidemics, poverty, the population explosion, women's literacy, family planning, birth control, decisions about abortion, and small business loans. In underdeveloped countries, small businesses consist of rabbit and pig farming, learning how to find water, and finding wood substitutes. Dobson objected to women's contention that gender roles were the result of societal and religious teaching. Certainly, he thought, women should not be allowed to talk about this to the world.

Some participants at the lecture and poetry reading on U.S. Chicanas had to stand in humid high temperatures vastly different from their own. Photograph by Sandra Romero.

REDEFINING THE GIRL CHILD

The majority of the roughly 30,000 women who met in China agreed that women allowed men to have too much influence on their lives. This process begins before a girl child is born, and it affects her until the day she dies. In many societies, males define what women wear, where they can go, what they can do, how they do it, and who they marry. They define how women adorn their bodies, how they walk and sit, who they pray to, and who they have sex with. Male dominance and the internalization of patriarchy have caused women to dislike their own lives, their bodies, and other women. Because of internalized patriarchy, women have gone on diets, experienced emotional collapses, acted as unpaid servants, been trafficked in as sex objects, and even committed suicide. Male attitude and influence in women's lives have subverted the feminist movement by demeaning female opinion and stifling the development of female consciousness. In many cases, men have made women afraid to become involved. The male need for control is so intense that, like the racist impulse, it frequently drives him to violence against women, thus making him highly emotionally impaired.

At the United Nations Fourth World Women's Conference, all of these subjects were discussed. Frequently, the issue of race was attached to other issues around the world because whiteness has been centralized in most countries around the world. Thus the so-called double whammy— the dual impact of gender and race on women's lives—changes. When to sexism and racism we add class discrimination, age bias, immigrant status, and physical or emotional impairment, then the victim is bombarded by several social blows, or intersecting variables (Figure 9.1). Intersecting variables cross over into one another, thereby compounding their impact. If the woman being affected is a lesbian woman of color, the affront to patriarchy is so intense that her very life is at risk.

Just as people of color have struggled in a world defined by whiteness, so women have struggled in a world bound together by patriarchy. Attempts to decentralize patriarchy, to remove the impact of men in women's lives, has not been holistic. This is why the attempts have made only small changes, but have failed to remove patriarchy at the center of civilization. The U.N. women's conference strives to diminish patriarchy. It is not clear that male world leaders recognize this tactic. Now that racism has been added to the platform, the next approach is to decentralize patriarchy and whiteness.

Most people believe that the feminist movement focuses on criticizing gender relations, specifically with men. On the contrary, it is about allowing women choice. Most women, and even men who desire greater choice in gender roles, don't want to confront male privilege. Most women are fearful that male abandonment and ridicule will destroy

Figure 9.1
Intersecting Variables

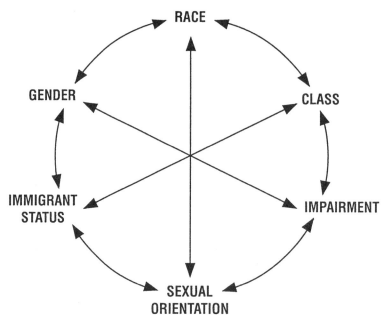

their respectable space in society. Women do not see their ridicule as psychological abuse. Furthermore, most women around the world are dependent on men to feed and clothe them as well as their children. These women are said to be abnegated women—women who willingly give up their happiness for the sake of others. But they are forced to give up their lives in exchange for meeting the needs of their children and for the comfort of men. One can only abnegate when there is choice; there is little choice in the matter. The only other acceptable choice for most is to not enter into relationships with men and endure the oppression of poverty and loneliness. Having same-sex relationships is not an option for these women.

Women have been bred to be ultrasensitive to mockery, sarcasm, and scorn. This can be so painful for women as to cause intimidation, lack of success, self-esteem, and motivation, and humiliation. Some women commit suicide in order to stop the pain. No one commits suicide because of one failure. Rather, it is frequently a series of small failures that cause women to lose interest in living. Many women fear living without a man, a male surname, a male income, a male network. This is why some women are against feminism. Feminism confronts patriarchy and seeks to ease that impact to allow females maximum freedom of choice. But daily relationships with men are but a minute part of the global movement. Rebuilding a global society is its real target. The movement includes some heterosexual elements, but other sexual elements of the movement encompass sexual orientation, lesbian relationships, and bi-sexuality. For the most part, the movement is about empowering women where they live, bettering the quality of their lives, easing the burden of unwaged labor, and redefining womanhood outside the confines of male dormancy.

Male insistence on controlling women has led many women to be kept as unpaid servants and women, generally unknowingly, have partici-pated in this master–servant plan. In China, for example, the tradition of binding girls' feet so that they would not grow large was (on the surface) done mostly to please men's aesthetic standards. It also pre-vented women's physical mobility. Interestingly, it was the child's mother who bound the feet, and the tradition went from mother to daughter generation after generation. Truly, women must be wary of the role they play in their own oppression.

One obvious arena in which men have played a prominent role is in that of beauty. Beauty as defined by white men has included the stan-dard of whiteness, thereby affecting the Chicana self-concept and self-worth, because Chicanas know they are not valued as beautiful women, especially if they are very dark or heavy. The label of "beautiful" is reserved for tall, lean, blond, blue-eyed women. Generally, Chicanas are neither tall, blond, nor blue-eyed; but many try to achieve this impossible standard by exercising, wearing high heels, using hair lighteners and hair dyes, wearing contact lenses, and using skin bleaches. Few can afford plastic surgery, as some Japanese women do who seek to westernize their eyes, and few know that the model of beauty is but an illusion. Even most white women cannot meet the standard.

Male-dominant social and religious norms have caused improvements in women's social status, usually in dollars and cents, when they get married. It changes again when these married women become mothers. But this gain is measured in social attitude only. Roles, values, and priv-ileges are generally superficial, causing women to gain only secondary adult status when married and when a child is born. She achieves the highest prestige when a boy child is delivered. In several countries, girl children are killed, abandoned, or put up for adoption. For years women around the globe have been chaperoned, lest some other man "get" to them. Women spend their lifetime walking behind men or on the build-ing side of him on the street. Avoiding this lifestyle is difficult and ex-pensive, and so is not an option.

LESBIAN ISSUES

Some speak of the "lesbian issue" as if it were isolated from the global women's movement. It is not. Because most women in the world are not free to select their own sexual partner, they are not free to select homosexuality. Thus, women are fearful of any inclination to respect and admire other women, leading some to become homophobic, fearing and even hating lesbians and lesbian relationships. Some women fear that they will become lesbians if they claim to be feminists or that people will think they are lesbians. What people think of them is more important than the right to choose sexual partners or to follow their natural inclinations as to sexual orientation. At the U.N. conference, women were not successful in getting into the final platform a statement that protected the rights of women who are lesbians.

Lesbians share in the Latina's racial and ethnic history. They, too, are impacted by class and gender discrimination. They share womanhood; they need to live out sexuality and define their own world and dreams. Among the most noted Chicana lesbians are Cherrie Moraga (1993), Emma Perez, Gloria Anzaldua, Ana Castillo, and Naomi Littlebear Moreno. These writers have given us some important insights into the Chicana feminist lesbian. They have explored the racism of the women's movement, the elitism of the gay movement, the benign cultural imperialism of the Latin American Solidarity movement, and the sexism of the Chicano movement. Cherrie Moraga (1993) notes that the Chicano movement could not embrace its *joteria* (gay population) in its quest for liberation. In some parts of the Chicano community Chicana lesbians have been given homophobic names like queer, butch, las otras, esas muchachas, tortierra, and maricona—all slurs degrading their sexual orientation and sexual preference. Males in the movement would not tolerate gays, and lesbians would not incorporate the issues into the movement. Raza, the "people," came first, the heterosexual people. Do not forget that feminists were also told to wait on behalf of "the people." Thus, only women who approved the heterosexual male liberation plan were "the people."

When Chicana lesbian feminism is reduced to humanism, it should not be subsumed in a secondary movement, but it has been, just as were Chicana feminists. Some Chicana feminists have had trouble allowing lesbians full participation in their movement. But Chicana/Latina lesbians and gay men do not merely seek inclusion in the Chicano nation: they seek to build a nation strong enough to embrace a full range of racial diversities, human sexualities, and expressions of gender. They believe their responsibility is to filter through the messages and create a life for the self. It is the societies' responsibility to not interfere. From the Chicano movement they seek a culture that can permit the natural expression of femaleness and maleness without prejudice or punishment (Moraga, 1993).

FEMINIST HEALTH CONCERNS

Every day Chicana lesbians and heterosexual Latinas die in secret. Breast cancer disproportionately affects the Latina lesbian community. It is popularly estimated that 74 percent of U.S. Latinas who needed mammograms in 1985 did not receive them. The statistic is high simply because physicians did not recommend the screening device. Age is a factor in self breast examination. Many do not perform the self-exam because physicians do not advise them to. In the 1980s, feminists pushed for treatment and prevention because it was estimated that breast cancer strikes one woman in nine. Often when it is diagnosed, it is in its late stages.

In 1992, 73 percent of all AIDS victims in the United States were Latinas. Many, believing this to be a gay and white disease, thought they were "safe." Rates are especially high among the homeless, prostitutes, the young and poor, and intravenous drug users (IVDU). A disproportionate number acquire the disease from their sexual partners, bisexual men. Puerto Ricans, Cubans, and Dominicans are widely afflicted as IVDUs. Chicanas and Latinas on the west coast tend to acquire AIDS through sexual relationships. Many Latinas believe that herbs like Uña de Gato (cat's claw) are a remedy for AIDS and cancer, but they are ineffective. This remedy is sold in male-owned herb stores, but women as well as men often prescribe.

Many abortion remedies are also available in herb stores. Many teen mothers continue to be cast out of their homes by their own parents who are shamed by their daughter's sexual irresponsibility. As in the colonial era, these women are not only punished but also isolated. Few have employment or medical insurance other than that provided by their parents. It is the parents who provide for the child, not the father of the child. The Chicano/Latino community is very embarrassed by the high teenage pregnancy rate. Non-Latinos do not want to support these children on welfare, and the fact that most of these teen girls are impregnated by older, legal-age men has fueled public support for legislation that mandates charging such men with rape or kidnapping if it appears that they have stolen, coerced, or seduced the girl. At this writing, no legal case testing this policy has yet gone to trial. Feminists continue to expose the sexual double standard that demands that women be virgins and dress in white when they marry. Feminists demand that it be noted that few women today are virgins and that men have rarely been virgins since colonial days.

As is true of sex and sexual orientation, health care has experienced some change with the inclusion of women. More women of color are needed to work with their populations. Some Chicanas are hesitant to pursue a career, or to be considered feminist because they desire to preserve family structure and family relationships. They fear interrupting the family, the culture, the high value for music, dance, cleanliness, and the ability to protect what they think they have in marriage. Chicana feminists, while working for the preservation of women's rights have remained critical of the family for what it does not provide. These are two different concerns. Because the national media do not cover this subject, and because the word "feminist" reeks of male bashing, white women, and lesbians, many Latinas have not joined feminists in their struggle for human rights within their own barrios. From this perspective, the U.N. women's conference and the globalization of the women's movement are very far away for them.

A statement frequently heard at the U.N. conference in 1995 was that men think women exist for their sexual pleasure. A little reported fact is that even in the United States women are frequently kidnapped for purposes of marriage. Latinos and Vietnamese in particular will "steal" a woman by keeping her out overnight, in order to force her into marrying when as a result of being out all night she is stigmatized as a "loose" woman. Women are also kidnapped and transported for sale or for prostitution purposes, or they are entrapped or imprisoned and forced to work, like the Vietnamese and Cambodian women who were forced to labor in El Monte, California. In 1995, it was discovered that these women were being held by men of their same background sewing clothing for sale at major, high-priced department stores. These women were said to be paying for their passage to the United States, but different circumstances arose so that they never finished paying. Only when the syndicate was raided by the police were these scared women freed.

Another little known fact is that Chinese women who do forced labor in China produce brand-name tennis shoes. In other instances, brand-name toys and electronic equipment are produced by girls no older than thirteen at a fraction of the cost for which it is sold in the United States. At the women's conference, there was much female testimony of having been sexually molested when they were girls, and of men demanding sex in return for jobs or job advancement. Some young girls run away to avoid sexual abuse, and many more of them die. A startling number commit suicide just to end the pain. Women have killed their bosses, their husbands, and their lovers in order to escape their brutality. Some, as several Latinas have confided in me, have even run away and immigrated to other countries, where they have been exploited in several other ways. Some have less choice. The men they are attached to—and their families, culture, laws, and religion—do not allow them even to consider ways of escaping. Molested and otherwise abused girls are only now beginning to seek treatment. Treatment is available because the global women's movement has pressured health institutions to provide it.

The foremost consideration with regard to women's health is how women participate in creating dependency on males for definition. Early pregnancy, for example, does not allow women to cultivate their talents and their social and other survival skills. Women, however, do not teach this dependency to their daughters alone. Early on, daughters learn that unaccompanied women are not physically safe in a man's world. But often they do not recognize when they are not emotionally and physically safe. Walking down the street subjects women to intimidation, insecurity, fear, and harassment. In addition to not demanding safe streets, Latinas feed the addiction to romance and personal and familial and gender strife by watching television novels. U.S. Latinas seem to be unaware that they teach their children to be super consumers when they allow them to watch too much television, spend too much money at Christmas, and take them to the mall and on other shopping trips. Few Latinas are aware that both men and women have been objectified for the sake of profit. Upwardly mobile women still look for men who can support them, and men still look for women who will allow themselves to be exhibited as proof of male prowess and self-worth. Males still demand sexual fidelity, and women cross their fingers and hope their men will not "cheat" on them or beat them.

THE NIÑO NETWORK

When I arrived in California in 1993, I was introduced to a new concept. The women there talked about the niño (infant) network in the context of gender relations. They referred to it as part of male attitude and behavior in higher education, as a reaction to women's art and literature, and in personal relationships. I gained more insight into it in China when a Mexican woman, who was also attending the conference, said, "Some men simply never mature emotionally." Since this woman was a therapist, I asked her what she meant. Her response was as follows: male psychosexual development is sometimes stunted. Their lack of maturity lies in their emotional inability to relate to women as equals. They remain fixated on ideas from their Spanish colonial past, when patriarchy ruled relatively unchallenged.

I explored this subject further with the feminists in California, and basically their perspective was that men grow up knowing they have certain privileges because they were born male. Boys witness adult male behavior, and how women traditionally respond to men, and assume this is the natural order in all situations. Mothers, sisters, and girlfriends reaffirm male privileged position, and within the context of love provide

Bicycles are a standard mode of Chinese transportation for both females and males. It is not uncommon to see three persons or heavy loads transported on a bicycle. Photograph by Irene I. Blea.

services to them. Males inappropriately believe that female servitude and nurturance outside of love relationships are to be expected of women. While love is not always political, it can have political ramifications. It is political when it is expected and when women are not honored, respected, and valued.

When women accept a secondary position, they compete for men and even cater to them. Girlfriends have ended friendships over men. Because of men, they will even physically fight, with the sole purpose of hurting other women. (Note the word girlfriend—as if these women never grow up either.)

Some husbands attempt to tear down their wife's self-esteem so that she will continue to try to serve him better. Males do this by simply comparing the wife to their mother or to other women. "No one makes tortillas like my mother." Translated this means, "You don't take care of me as well as my mother did," "You are not a good service provider." Some men are more cruel. They isolate the woman by taking her to live outside her familial network, or they purposefully manipulate estrangement from the family. They degrade her women friends or try to seduce those friends. Some men hit or beat their wives, and then deny it. This behavior obscures the fact that such men are highly female dependent or inappropriately self-identified.

Anthropologist Sam Rios at California State University in Sacramento contends that men's maturity level can be measured by simply asking what age they were when they bought and washed their own underwear. Generally, a man never does his own wash: first his mama and then his girlfriend or wife does it.

No serious examination of the male gender role among heterosexual males took place until the controversial Million Man March in New York City in 1996. There was some discussion among Chicano males of organizing such a march in Denver, Colorado, along with African-American males. The fact is that males need to reflect on their own lives, and hopefully engage in serious dialogue and writing so that a serious academic discourse can be conducted by both males and females.

Men need to do their own research on men. They need to deal with the fact that many groups of women believe that men are not sufficiently mature to be able to form healthy relationships with strong, intelligent women. So many men have improperly idealized images of women and are childlike. The niño network is an extension of the idea that the traditional Latina is defined and controlled by male influence in her socialization process, which ends only when she acquiesces to male expectations. The consequences of deviating from prescribed gender roles, and the appearance of Chicanas and other Latinas on the national scene, are threatening to the male sense of self because he has such a false sense of self.

At the professional and perhaps at the personal level too, the niño network gives a false sense of power based on emotional stuntedness that demands that women be barred from professional activities. They need to function as gatekeepers and power brokers because they have institutionalized their perception of reality and have corrupted the liberation process. They need, in the psychological sense, recognition as men of power. This false sense of power role allows them to penetrate female space. Some have even appropriated Chicana feminist scholarship to act in a politically correct fashion, but women know they are insincere.

Since Chicana/Latina feminism has a firm base in academia, the niño network should be examined in that context. At the university, many students avoid Chicana courses in Chicano Studies out of fear of indoctrination. Specifically, they fear they will be exposed to lesbian sex. Some advisors and non-Chicano faculty also believe that the courses offered are not academically strong. Members of traditional education fear that the courses question and directly challenge the social and political use of a white, male-dominant education. To teach Latinas and Chicanas that there are intelligent, strong role models who generally are not highly visible in their homes becomes a political activity. Both females and males are not aware that music, poetry and art speak to them about women. They avoid meeting women like Chicana and Latina cultural artists Judy Baca and Yrina Cervantes, seeing the films of Lourdes Portillo or Solame Espana, hearing the poetry of Lorna Dee Cervantes, or attending plays written by Josefina Lopez, Evelina Fernandez, Edit Villareal, or Cherrie Moraga. Moraga asserts that gay and lesbian images are still taboo (1993). Millions of women are denied knowledge because certain information does not enter their homes or schools, and because the men in their lives are repulsed by feminist thought.

The question that arises then is, how does this exclusion manifest itself in education, especially higher education, where patriarchy and whiteness are centralized and where "scholars" do not take Chicana scholarship seriously? Apparently, males do not have a good understanding of the intersection of colonialism and patriarchy. This lack of understanding is not just disadvantageous to women: in addition, the Chicano community is cheated when individuals do not give serious attention to persons attempting to empower the community by empowering themselves. Male inability to recognize the intersection of variables in their own lives is evident in Chicana art and other forms of creativity.

Chicana creativity is not taken seriously. Sandra Cisneros, a Chicana writer, refers to this reaction as the "that's good mi hija" syndrome. Mothers and fathers who do not understand the nature of young Chicana artistic productions will say, "That's good mi hija" thereby patronizing the work and not actively supporting its continuation. Men do the same thing as part of ensuring that their network of dominance is not interrupted by Chicanas saying this can no longer be. But Chicanas have challenged the network. Chicanas and lesbian feminists have ruptured the net by continuing to define their own lives. Men now have to grow up and learn how to take care of their own personal needs. Basic social-economic realities now demand that Chicanos rely on Chicanas to work outside the home in order to support households. Most men cannot do it alone today. Female incomes can no longer simply purchase the extras. Now they purchase the necessities of life: food, clothing, and shelter. A Chicano can no longer expect a Chicana to work and provide a full range of free domestic services while working outside the home and having his children in order to ensure that his "name" will continue. Feminists no longer want to entertain a spouse's friends and family, socialize with his fellow workers, work outside the home, have his children, and provide a full range of unpaid domestic services. Men have differentiated between women who are willing to do this and those who will not. They now need to learn that gender relationships cannot happen on their terms, based on their time line.

Chicana feminists have lost patience with men. They no longer want to teach them and spoon feed them information about how to live with women in truly meaningful relationships. Men have to admit their dependency on women and figure out how to complete their psychosexual development and mature on their own. They, or their parents, or the educational institutions around the country, have to teach men appropriate gender behavior, bring them to a level of understanding about the nature of their sexism, their surface support versus their genuine support; or they will live practicing serial monogamy. Women are busy teaching other women that there is another way to live; that the last thing a bright, energetic, creative Chicana would want to do would be to align herself with a man who expects domestic services, considers her income incidental to their lifestyle, says "That's good mi hija," or calls her "mammy," and thinks of her as a baby-making machine that produces and raises "his" sons to carry on his name. Believe it or not, some men still measure their manhood by the services and children that women provide them free of charge and by the number of legitimate and illegitimate children they have. They use these women and later walk away making it difficult for them to receive economic and other child support.

If this scenario is not true, then Chicano males need to deal with those situations that make it true for so many Chicanas, just as they need to deal with the fact that women are tired of seeing so many Chicano men kill other Chicano men. According to recent statistics on American violence, Latinos kill and hurt one another at a much higher rate then Anglos kill and physically hurt Chicanos or even other Anglo males. While these men are so busy killing one another, they are shooting innocent women and children. According to the Los Angeles Police Department, more young Chicanos die as a result of guns than by automobile accident, drug and alcohol use, and natural causes. The same is true for African American and American Indian men. Certainly, racism plays a role, but so does sexism because it is not true of women in general. Chicano males and other males of color have to discover how they have internalized racism and sexism before they can stop the adolescent tendency to solve their problems through violence.

Women are encouraging other women not to get involved with such men. They are beginning to realize that they are paying for the cost of policing, representing, and jailing these men (Stephenson, 1991). They can, and they do, advocate for men, but when men do not take women seriously in other arenas women allow them to "stew in their own mess." Only men can end their own violent oppression, and they cannot end it by leaving places where violence of any kind takes place because it is just about everywhere. If they succeed in leaving their communities, they abandon the community that worked so hard to make it possible for them to leave in the first place. This becomes an ethical issue, one that the community will judge. Those men who value community, who truly are Chicano, who continue to work to empower their community by empowering their women, and themselves, need to be more informed and vocal about the impact of sexism on the lives of Chicano males. And in union with women, they need to take action to correct what is stifling Chicano and Latino communities.

LINKING KNOWLEDGE TO POWER AND ACTION

For Chicanas, the search for power can begin by concentrating on contemporary social and political issues that should not receive attention in historical isolation or separate from issues that impact women. This search for power should recognize that many women have been thrown into leadership roles because of their personal circumstances. After finding themselves in these leadership positions, most have made a conscious choice to inform themselves. They have acknowledged that leadership does not mean one leader, but a leadership pool, a shared leadership. In their choices they have resisted English as the official language of the United States, but male leaders who would not share the leadership did not lend a gender perspective to their analysis, and in some states lost the legal right to have some forms of public communication in Spanish.

Many women were involved in Proposition 187, granting social services to those who could not prove citizenship, and the Leticia A and Bradford decisions, curtailing educational access to those who could not prove U.S. citizenship in California. Once again, male leaders would not share the leadership with women (the California system has more female than male students), or enter into a gender analysis. As a result, undocumented Latinos and Latinas lost the right to attend the university through financial aid. White male attacks on Affirmative Action need a Chicana/Latina perspective. When Chicanas and Latinas resisted Proposition 187 in 1989, they did so because roughly half of the Latino population growth in the state was due to Mexican immigration across what was considered an imperialist-imposed border in northern Mexico. Furthermore, they believed that human beings have the right to food, shelter, and medicine in any country. The U.S. Immigration and Naturalization Service estimated that 1.2 million apprehensions were made at the Mexican border that year. Many of the immigration officials violated the human rights of those crossing the illegal border. The Leticia A and Bradford decisions and Proposition 187 placed women at the front line, acting as the policing agent as they served as school secretaries and teachers and hospital clerical workers and nurses.

Chicanas and other Latinas have opposed NAFTA, which they believe victimized primarily women in maquiladoras (border factories) when U.S. production moved to Mexico to maximize its profit. The U.S.-Mexican border is an appealing site because women provide a cheap army of labor. Mexico has reaped little benefit, whereas U.S. corporations have been able to avoid paying U.S. taxes, a decent daily wage, and health or retirement benefits to workers. A maquiladora worker earned about $3.40 per day in 1988; she earned $3.75 in 1992; and it is estimated that in 1996 she earned $3.85. Work involving dangerous and unregulated substances exposes women to hazardous chemicals and conditions. Many fear that through NAFTA, multinational investors inherited the most economically efficient connection between global ecological exploitation, devastation, and the drive to expand markets by creating a demand for U.S. white male-controlled commodities like clothing, technology, automobiles, and food. Some of these products are harmful to human beings.

Immigration from underdeveloped countries to highly developed Western countries has accelerated during the past quarter century among those seeking higher education and employment. Many of those who do not immigrate migrate to distant towns and cities in search of wage labor. There they are exploited. Some return home at regular intervals, but others never return. This is true of Mexican women who work in maquiladoras. Women constitute at least half of the textile workers in Puerto Rico and El Salvador and are the majority in the United States as agricultural workers, packing strawberries and harvesting flowers. Owners and managers report they do not like to hire men to do the monotonous work of women (Fisher, 1989, p. 99) According to Maxine Fisher, if given a choice, young women between the ages of fifteen and twenty-four who are unmarried prefer to work in the packing plants. Their intense economic needs, plus their passive attitude toward working in factories, is one of the main reasons why multinational corporations give 80 to 90 percent of their low-paying and semiskilled assembly-line jobs to women. A personnel manager of one such corporation reported to Fisher that young men were too restless to work in the factories. If they were displeased, they would sabotage machines and threaten the foreman; at most, all girls would do was cry a little.

Indigenous women do not immigrate to the United States in great numbers largely because of the cost of immigration. Mistecas, Oaxacan Indians, for example, have to finance the immigration of another according to social and religious custom. Some financing is done in dollars, and some is done in pesos. Certain segments of U.S. agriculture are becoming "indigenized," that is, becoming more Indian. With regard to gender among the indigenous and other immigrants, much about the immigration process remains obscure, especially in the area of reproduction and spousal and partnered relationships. What is known is that the expectations of what the United States is like are very different from the reality. Immigrants do not expect to endure exploitation, sexism, and racism. Many immigrant Latinas do not understand why they experience racism in the United States because they do not know the history of Chicanos in that country and the fact that they have inherited this legacy. Most U.S. Chicanas do not even know the roots of their colonialization and how the immigrant Latina inherits the Chicana legacy when she enters the United States. Frequently, Chicanas discriminate against immigrants, treating them as aliens, intruders, and invaders wanting Chicana and Chicano jobs, which are the lowest paid, least protected form of employment in the country. Those who discriminate have internalized most americanization teachings. Those Chicanas who welcome their Latino sisters and brothers into occupied Mexico strive to teach them the Chicana legacy of white patriarchy.

The newly arrived women do not represent more poverty to an already impoverished population. They do not represent more stereotypes to an already overstereotyped group of women. Those who welcome immigrant women and men recognize that Latina and Latino immigration makes cultural contributions to a land that should not only boast about its multiculturalism, but also should incorporate into it a perspective that goes beyond what immigrants have done to revive the economy in the United States by providing cheap labor. Indeed, immigration enriches U.S. culture with more and different linguistic traditions, forms of knowledge, music, dance, food, medicine, religion, justice, and alternative ways of thinking and doing things.

The 1995 U.N. conference on women focused on this diversity, which does not dilute the painful realities of people of color. Knowing that China has had a long tradition of killing girl babies, giving them up for adoption, or simply abandoning them creates a sisterhood among women. Knowing that parts of Africa have long practiced female clitoral mutilation also creates a sisterhood. One objective of the conference was to increase the value of girl children in women's eyes, and in the eyes of the world generally, and to educate them based on balancing power between the sexes and persons of different sexual orientation. The conference strove to impress governments as to the importance of raising girls with their rights guaranteed. That is, they should have the right to grow up free from physical mutilation and emotional and spiritual damage; they have the right to know about the freedom to choose their own sexual and marital partners; they have to right to decide whether they will have and raise babies; and they have the right to speak about their concerns as women. After women returned from China, they participated in a worldwide information campaign known as Beyond Beijing. This campaign takes the U.N. platform and other work done in China directly to women where they live. In the United States this includes Indian reservations, black ghettos, and Latino barrios.

The conference made concrete the fact that women have changed and

Sisters smile for the camera. Photograph by Oscar Castillo.

are going to change even more. Thus, culture has changed and will continue to change. And so too will men. Politically sophisticated males know that women outnumber men in the world and that in order to get female support for their political and economic agendas they should at least talk about women's issues. The world has changed, so that conscientious young men are helping to rear children by participating in their delivery and their everyday care. More men are supporting female artistic production than ever before. And some religions are even beginning to see the value of women's roles and are integrating them into the fabric of their organizations. The time of "normal" activity for women has passed, and the norm has been redefined by feminists around the world, who have gained power through knowledge linked to action.

Chicana scholars have served as the academic arm of the Chicana feminist movement, but these women are also highly involved in their community. They have striven to politicize education by designing and offering courses on la Chicana. In the late 1980s, a young woman by the name of Rosalia Gonzales read a book entitled *La Chicana and the Intersection of Race, Class, and Gender* (Blea, 1991). In 1995, she and Esperanza Velen designed a program to teach Chicana feminism in the community through an alternative education project. This and other projects targeting Latina women have furthered the goals of Chicana feminism. Not wishing to create an imbalance between mothers and daughters, Velen and Gonzales had the sensitivity to work with the parents. Thus, both mothers and daughters, as well as a few fathers, are becoming more feminist.

Chicanas complain that white feminist faculty, who have devoted years to Women's Studies, have taken too long to effectively deal with their racism. They are hesitant to move Latinas into tenured full-time positions in Women's Studies and in other departments. University students are rarely exposed to a Chicana professor outside of Chicano Studies, and only recently in Women's Studies. University students complain of sexual harassment by male faculty, but sexual harassment takes place even on the elementary school ground where boys still lift girls' dresses, attempt to peek into the girls' gym, and try to touch girls' developing breasts.

Chicana feminist criticism now analyzes power relationships at both national and international levels. It frequently identifies itself with the struggles of underdeveloped countries and strives to transform institutions. But transforming institutions requires time. U.S. Latinas are highly resilient and tenacious. Cultural and historical social conditions have demanded that females develop strong characters and engage in hard labor, especially when it comes to living out their value of homeland in the arid southwest. Casual observation of women in many Chicano neighborhoods reveals that heterosexual women are not hesitant to work alongside men in maintaining their home, educating children, creating a garden, or contributing to their community in dry, hot conditions in summer and very cold winters (Blea, 1991). For the most part, they make good employees because they have internalized a work ethic that is somewhat stronger than the dominant work ethic, for in order to have what they have they have to work harder.

Chicana feminists understand that Chicano males have endured discrimination, which has served to emasculate them, to rob them of their self-esteem, and to deny them jobs. But they also know that many men have abandoned women and children, and so they are searching for a new definition of manhood. Latina feminists are aware that men have been given preferential positions and treatment in Chicano culture. This tendency did not begin with Anglo political imposition in 1848, but was more heartily embraced by men after the imposition of the U.S. government. This imposition and the accompanying racism played a key role in emasculating Chicano men. Sexism is one of the last straws grasped at by Chicano males in an effort to sustain male power.

Different expectations from Latinas require different responses from men. Simply put, Chicanas are forcing men to not live down to a standard. Men, like dominant Americans, will have to accept the idea that Latinas are their equal, are fluent in two (even three) cultures and a minimum of two languages, and that Latinas frequently outperform them. Chicanas recognize that many Chicanos are unfortunately afflicted by the symptoms of discrimination: prison, gangs, poverty, drugs, early fatherhood, crowded housing, bad health, environmental hazards, and all of the stereotypes, but so are women, and women can no longer wait for men. They are developing a consciousness that cannot be explained by the internal colonial model of oppression. They are going beyond a call for decolonization, and they are doing it for themselves because they have learned that their oppressor will not. It is men who must liberate themselves from patriarchy. The Latina has set the base.

REFERENCES

Blea, Irene I. 1991. *La Chicana and the Intersection of Race, Class, and Gender*. New York: Praeger.

———. 1991. *Bessemer: A Sociological Perspective of a Chicano Barrio*. New York: AMS Press.

Fisher, Maxine P. 1989. *Women in the Third World*. New York: Franklin Watts.

Moraga, Cherrie. 1993. *The Last Generation*. Boston: South End Press.

Snortland, Ellen. 1995, July 21, "Dobson," *Pasadena Weekly*, p. 35.

Stephenson, June. 1991. *Men Are Not Cost-Effective*. New York: HarperPerennial.

SELECTED BIBLIOGRAPHY

Acuna, Rodolfo. 1988. *Occupied America: A History of Chicanos*. 3rd ed. New York: Harper and Row.

Anaya, Rudolfo A. 1986. *Chicano in China*. Albuquerque: University of New Mexico Press.

Anaya, Rudolfo A., and Francisco A. Lomeli, eds. 1991. *Aztlan: Essays on the Chicano Homeland*. Albuquerque: University of New Mexico Press.

Associated Press. 1990. *China: From the Long March to Tiananmen Square*. New York: Henry Holt and Co.

Baca-Zinn, Maxine. 1975. "Political Familism: Toward Sex Role Equality in Chicano Families." *Aztlan: Chicano Journal of the Social Sciences and the Arts* 6 (Spring): 19–31.

———. 1975. "Chicanas: Power and Control in the Domestic Sphere." *De colores* 1, No. 3: 13–26.

Baca-Zinn, Maxine, Lynn Cannon, Elizabeth Higgenbotham, and Bonnie Thorton Dill. 1986. "The Costs of Exclusionary Practices in Women's Studies." *Signs: Journal of Women in Culture and Society*, 2, No. 21.

Baez, Joan. 1966. *Daybreak*. New York: Avon.

Balderama, Francisco E., and Raymond Rodriguez. 1994. *Decade of Betrayal: Mexican Repatriation in the 1930s*. Albuquerque: University of New Mexico Press.

Barrera, Mario. 1979. *Race and Class in the Southwest*. Notre Dame, Ind.: University of Notre Dame Press.

Blauner, Robert. 1969. "Internal Colonialism and Ghetto Revolt." *Social Problems* 16 (Spring): 393–408.

Blea, Irene I. 1988. *Toward a Chicano Social Science*. New York: Praeger.

———. 1991. *Bessemer: A Sociological Perspective of a Chicano Barrio*. New York: AMS Press.

———. 1991. *La Chicana and the Intersection of Race, Class and Gender*. New York: Praeger.

———. 1995. *Researching Chicano Communities: Social-Historical, Physical, Psychological, and Spiritual Space*. New York: Praeger.

Branch, Louis Leon. 1980. *Los Bilitos: The Story of Billy the Kid and His Gang*. New York: Carlton Press.

Cabeza de Baca, Fabiola. 1954. *We Fed Them Cactus*. Albuquerque: University of New Mexico Press.

Cammermeyer, Margarethe, and Chris Fisher. 1994. *Serving in Silence*. New York: Viking. New York: Recorded Books, Inc.

Castillo, Ana. 1995. *Massacre of the Dreamers: Essays on Xicanisma*. Albuquerque: University of New Mexico Press.

Cheng, Nien. 1987. *Life and Death in Shanghai*. New York: Grove Press, Books on Tape, 1987.

Chronicle of America. 1993. Mount Kisco, N.Y.: Chronicle Publications.

Coser, Lewis A. 1959. *The Function of Social Conflict*. Glencoe, Ill.: Free Press.

Cotera, Martha. 1976. *Diosa y Hembra*. Austin, Tex.: Information Systems Development.

Dahrendorf, Ralf. 1959. *Class and Class Conflict in Industrial Society*. Stanford, Calif.: Stanford University Press.

Dale, Bruce, and Joel Sartore. 1996, February. "Tex Mex Border." *National Geographic*, pp. 44–69.

Diaz, Rose. 1992. "Lola Chavez de Armijo, 1858–1929." In ed., Tey Diana Rebolledo, *Nuestra Mujeres*. Albuquerque: University of New Mexico Press.

Díaz (del Castillo), Bernal. 1963. *The Conquest of New Spain*. Trans. J. M. Cohen. New York: Penguin Books.

Durkheim, Emile. 1915. *The Elementary Forms of the Religious Life*. New York: Macmillan and Free Press. (Originally published in 1897.)

———. 1964. *The Division of Labor in Society*. Translated by George Simpson. New York: Macmillan and Free Press. (Originally published in 1893.)

Encuentro Femenil. 1974. *Encuentro Femenil: The First Chicana Feminist Journal*. Los Angeles: Hijas de Cuauhtemoc.

Enriquez, Evangelina, and Alfredo Mirande. 1979. *La Chicana: The Mexican American Woman*. Chicago: University of Chicago Press.

Fannon, Franz. 1963. *The Wretched of the Earth*. New York: Grove Press.

Figueroa Torres, J. Jesus. 1975. *Doña Marina: Una India Ejemplar*. Mexico. D.F.: Ed: B. Costa-Amic.

Fisher, Maxine P. 1989. *Women in the Third World*. New York: Franklin Watts.

Garcia, John, Julia Curry Rodriguez, and Clara Lomas, eds. 1988. *Times of Challenge: Chicanos and Chicanas in American Society*. Houston: University of Houston Press, Mexican American Studies Program, Monograph Series No. 6.

Gomez-Quinones, Juan. 1990. *Chicano Politics: Reality and Promise, 1940–1990.* Albuquerque: University of New Mexico Press.

———. 1990. "Chicano Politics." *La Raza Magazine.* Vol. 2. Albuquerque: University of New Mexico Press.

———. 1990. "Patsy Tijerina on Suspended Sentence, But It's Our Land." *La Raza Magazine*, Vol. 2, pp. 16–19.

Gomez-Tagle, Silvia, Adrian Garcia Valdes, and Lourdes Grobet. 1985. *National Museum of Anthropology: Mexico.* Trans. Joan Ingram-Eiser. Distribución Cultural Especializada.

Harrington, Michael. 1963. *The Other American: Poverty in the United States.* Baltimore, Md.: Penguin.

Harrison, Paul. 1981. *Inside the Third World.* New York: Penguin Books.

Heller, Celia. 1966. *Mexican American Youth: Forgotten Youth at the Crossroads.* New York: Random House.

Hernández, Deluvina. 1970. *Mexican American Challenge to a Sacred Cow.* Los Angeles: Chicano Cultural Center.

Hotz, Robert Lee. 1995. "Is Concept of Race a Relic?" *Los Angeles Times*, April 15, 1995, pp. 1, 14.

Jaramillo, Cleofas. 1939. *Cuentos del Hogar.* El Campo, Tex.: Citizen Press. Reprinted 1942. Santa Fe, N. Mex.: Seton Village Press.

———. 1941. *Sombras del Pasado/Shadows of the Past.* Santa Fe, N. Mex.: Ancient City Press.

———. 1955. *Romance of a Little Village Girl.* San Antonio, Tex.: Naylor.

Kluckhohn, Florence, and Fred L. Strodbeck. 1961. *Variations in Value Orientations.* Evanston, Ill.: Row Peterson.

Lammana, Richard, and Julian Samora. 1967. *Mexican Americans in a Midwest Metropolis: A Study of East Chicago.* Los Angeles: Mexican American Project.

Marx, Karl, and Friedrich Engels. 1955. *Communist Manifesto.* Chicago: H. Regnery Co.

Marx, Karl, and Friedrich Engels. 1965. "The Communist Manifesto." In Arthur Mendel, ed., *Essential Works of Marxism.* New York: Bantam Books. (Original work published in 1848.)

McWilliams, Carey. 1939. *Factories in the Field: The Story of Migratory Farm Labor in California.* Boston: Little, Brown, and Co.

———. 1968. *North from Mexico: The Spanish-Speaking People of the United States.* New York: Greenwood Press. (Originally printed in 1949.)

Mead, Margaret. 1935. *Sex and Temperament in Three Primitive Societies.* New York: William Morrow.

Medsen, William. 1964. *Mexican Americans of South Texas.* New York: Holt, Rinehart and Winston.

Melville, Margaritta B. 1980. *Twice a Minority*, St. Louis: C. V. Mosby Press.

Memmi, Albert. 1965. *The Colonizer and the Colonized.* Boston: Beacon Press.

Moore, Thomas. 1992. *Care of the Soul.* New York: HarperCollins. Recorded Books, 1994.

Moraga, Cherrie. 1993. *The Last Generation.* Boston: South End Press.

National Women's History Project. 1992. "Adelante Mujeres." (Video) Washington, D.C.

Padilla, Genaro M. 1993. *My History, Not Yours: The Formation of Mexican-American Autobiography*. Madison: University of Wisconsin Press.

Parsons, Talcott. 1951. *Essays on Sociological Theory*. Glencoe, Ill.: Free Press.

Paz, Octavio. 1961. *Labyrinth of Solitude*. New York: Grove Press.

Pu Yi, Aisin-Gioro. 1989. *From Emperor to Citizen: The Autobiography of Aisin-Gioro Pu Yi*. Beijing: Foreign Language Press.

Romano, Octavio. 1968. "The Anthropology and Sociology of the Mexican Americans: The Distortion of Mexican-American History." *El Grito* (Fall), pp. 13–26.

Snortland, Ellen. 1995, July 21. "Focus on Dobson." *Pasadena Weekly*, p.10.

Stephenson, June. 1991. *Men Are Not Cost-Effective*. New York: HarperPerennial.

Swadesh, Frances Leon. 1974. *Los Primeros Pobladores*. South Bend, Ind.: University of Notre Dame Press.

Torres-Gill, Fernando M. 1992. *The New Aging: Politics and Change in America*. Westport, Conn.: Auburn House.

Trujillo, Marcella Lucero. 1975, March 12–16. "The Road to Canon: The Road to La Pinta." *An Anthology of Chicano Literature*. Austin, Tex.: Chicano Studies Center.

Tuchman, Barbara Wertheim. 1986. *Notes from China*. Charlotte Hall, Md.: Recorded Books, 1986.

Tuck, Ruth. 1946. *Not with the Fist: Mexican Americans in a Southwest City*. New York: Harcourt, Brace and Co.

United Nations Department of Public Information. 1985. "World Survey on the Role of Women in Development." Report, p. 93. Recorded in *Review and Appraisal*. New York.

U.S. Department of Commerce, Bureau of the Census. 1993, April. *American Demographics*. Washington, D.C.: Government Printing Office.

U.S. Department of Commerce, Economics and Statistics Administration, Bureau of the Census. 1993, November. *We the American Hispanics*. Washington, D.C.: Government Printing Office.

Veyna, Angelina F. 1986. "Women in Early New Mexico: A Preliminary View." In T. Cordova et al., eds., *Chicana Voices: Intersections of Class, Race and Gender*. Austin: CMAS Publications, University of Texas Press.

Weitz, Shirley. 1977. *Sex Roles: Biological, Psychological, and Social Function*. New York: Oxford University Press.

Willoya, William, and Vinson Brown. 1962. *Warriors of the Rainbow: Strange and Prophetic Dreams of the Indians*. Happy Camp, Calif.: Naturegraph Co.

Ybarra, Leonarda. 1982, February. "When Wives Work: The Impact on the Chicano Family." *Journal of Marriage and the Family*, No. 44, pp. 169–178.

———. "Conjugal Role Relationships in the Chicano Family." Ph.D. diss., University of California, Berkeley.

INDEX

About the Author

IRENE I. BLEA is Chairperson of the Chicano Studies Department, California State University, Los Angeles. A well-respected scholar of Latino life and culture, she has published extensively, including *Toward a Chicano Social Science* (Praeger, 1988), *La Chicana and the Intersection of Race, Class, and Gender* (Praeger, 1991), and *Researching Chicano Communities* (Praeger, 1995).

ISBN 0-275-95623-7

HARDCOVER BAR CODE